Wakefield Press

OUR FATHERS CLEARED THE BUSH

Jill Roe AO was born at Tumby Bay on South Australia's Eyre Peninsula and spent her first fourteen years living on the Peninsula. She is Professor Emerita in Modern History at Macquarie University, Sydney, where she was awarded a DLitt as a higher research degree for her work on Australian writer Miles Franklin, principally the Margarey Medal-winning *Stella Miles Franklin: A Biography.* Her publications in Australian social and cultural history include numerous entries in the *Australian Dictionary of Biography* and *The Wakefield Companion to South Australian History.*

Jill Roe lives at Pearl Beach on the Central Coast of NSW.

By the same author

Stella Miles Franklin: A Biography

My Congenials: Miles Franklin and Friends in Letters, 1879–1954

Beyond Belief: Theosophy in Australia 1879–1939

Marvellous Melbourne: The Emergence of an Australian City

Our Fathers Cleared the Bush

Remembering Eyre Peninsula

JILL ROE

Wakefield Press

Wakefield Press
16 Rose Street
Mile End
South Australia 5031
www.wakefieldpress.com.au

First published 2016

Cover designed by Liz Nicholson, designBITE
Edited by Emily Hart, Wakefield Press
Typeset by Wakefield Press

National Library of Australia Cataloguing-in-Publication entry

Creator:	Roe, Jill, 1940- , author.
Title:	Our fathers cleared the bush: remembering Eyre Peninsula / Jill Roe.
ISBN:	978 1 74305 429 1 (paperback).
Notes:	Includes index.
Subjects:	Country life - South Australia - Eyre Peninsula - Ancedotes. Eyre Peninsula (S.A.) - History. Eyre Peninsula (S.A.) - Social life and customs - Ancedotes.
Dewey Number:	994.238

Wakefield Press thanks Coriole Vineyards for their continued support.

CONTENTS

For my sisters, Pauline, Jean, and Heather,

and in memory of my old friend the late Helen Bartley ('Woodie'),

with whom I shared an Eyre Peninsula childhood.

Introduction

The origins of this book lie in my now distant childhood. I was born at Tumby Bay on Lower Eyre Peninsula, South Australia, a farmer's daughter who, for reasons touched upon in the following pages, was sent away to school in the city in 1955, as it turned out for good. There, in order to meet the requirements of school geography, I first researched aspects of the Eyre Peninsula story. This I did with enthusiasm. However, at university my interests shifted from geography to history and in due course I became a historian.

In this book, written in later life and with a renewed sense of place, I include my own experience where it seems relevant. The aim is not so much to tell my own story – though I often start there – nor to fill a gap in the literature – though there is one – but rather, on the basis of personal recollections and a now quite extensive range of materials, to capture some key aspects of, and moments in, the regional experience over time.

The writing dates from 2011. It was time to make a start. Inevitably, the question first put to me by historian Manning Clark in the 1960s – 'what have you go to say?' – has loomed large. At that time, I had no answer: 'Who? Me?' I thought. Nor did I have a viable perspective. However, by now it is a case of 'better late than never', and there's been plenty of time to gain a perspective.

The book has 10 chapters which run in a roughly chronological sequence, from the earliest times to more or less the present day. Seven are newly researched and, as indicated in notes, three have been previously published and are here subject to minor editing. As well, at the suggestion of colleagues, I have added as a prologue a previously published account of my early years.

Acknowledgements

For help with Chapter 7, I would like to acknowledge Robyn Arrowsmith, Jane Connors, Pat Green, Marnie Hughes-Warrington, Nick Price, and Jean Robb, also the Australian History Museum, Macquarie University, the Mitchell Library, and the Powerhouse Museum, Sydney, for assistance with research for the South Australian History Council's Annual Lecture of 13 May 2005, for which this chapter was originally written. The lecture was published in the *Journal of the Historical Society of South Australia*, 34, 2006, pages 1–10.

The Prologue was first published in 'First Matriculate . . .', *Against the Odds: Fifteen professional women reflect on their lives and careers*, 1983, pages 58–63.

For encouragement and support during the research and writing, I thank Margaret Allen, Margaret Bettison, Peggy Brock, David Carment, Baiba Berzins, Chris Cunneen, Desley Deacon, Pat Green, Maureen Heath, Beverley Kingston, Jean Robb, David Floyd Smith, Andrew Robb, Andrew and Jennie Strickland, and my colleagues at Macquarie University and the University of Adelaide.

These chapters are extensively illustrated. For this I offer a grateful general acknowledgement in addition to those that appear with the graphics. A special acknowledgement is made to Adelaide artist Annie Newmarch: the title of the book comes from an early work of hers, a print of which I was fortunate to obtain many years ago. As well,

I especially thank the Mitchell Library in Sydney, the State Library of South Australia in Adelaide, the National Library of Australia in Canberra, and the municipal library in Port Lincoln, for access to materials in their care.

Several illustrations are taken from publications. These are credited briefly in the captions. The full references are:

'The Personal Touch'
The Personal Touch: A look at South Australia's Postal History, Julie Green, Australia Post, 1986 pages 23, 24

'Gum Trees and Gullies'
Gum Trees and Gullies, Yallunda Flat Book Committee, 1986 pages 89, 97, 129

'Grains of Mustard Seed'
Grains of Mustard Seed, Colin Thiele, Education Department of SA, 1975 page 106

'Hauling the Load'
Hauling the Load: A history of Australia's working horses and bullocks, Malcolm Kennedy, Melbourne University Press, 1992 page 118

'Wildflowers of Lower Eyre Peninsula'
Wildflowers of Lower Eyre Peninsula, Ursula Halls, Australian Plants Society, 2001 page 122

'Natural History of Eyre Peninsula'
Natural History of Eyre Peninsula, Twidale, Tyler and Davies, Royal Society of South Australia, 1985 page 187

PROLOGUE

The formative years of my life were spent in the farming communities of Eyre Peninsula on the west coast of South Australia. I was born at Tumby Bay on Spencer Gulf in November 1940, the daughter of John Roe, farmer, and Edna Ivy, nee Heath, nurse and housewife. I left Eyre Peninsula in early 1955 for further schooling in Adelaide.

Current wisdom has it that mothers are the most important factor in shaping girls' ambitions. This is dubious historically and, in my case, perforce untrue. My mother died on 13 January 1942 in a private hospital in Adelaide after a long illness when I was fourteen months old. She died, in the words of the death certificate, of 'pulmonary tuberculosis, some months', or, as her sister said grimly, of washing too many sheets. In today's terms, it was a preventable death. Had the necessary antibiotics been available, she may have recovered, despite four pregnancies in seven years and vulnerability to tuberculosis, which had already carried off one of her sisters. In historical terms, it was a death of its time, a late instance of the appalling rate of maternal mortality prevailing in Australia until the late 1940s, also evidence of the deprivation of the Great Depression as it affected small wheat farmers on the edge of subsistence.

Perhaps the stigma then surrounding tuberculosis as a 'dirty disease' helped those close to her to contain their grief. A certain stoic realism – or was it reticence? – attended the rare recollection of Edna Roe by relatives in my early childhood. I knew what I was told, which wasn't much: that she had been a trained nurse, a hard worker, that perfectionism was her downfall. My father very sensibly discouraged morbid introspection, and never discussed her himself, though a perplexing Ascension print hung over his bed, and a large polished wood glory box stood in the bedroom corner. The rarely disclosed contents of this box provided an occasional diversion on wet days, especially for my second sister, Jean, who also suffered afflictions characteristic of the period, valiantly surmounting what was long thought to be infantile paralysis and only recently recognised as a birth injury. I made do with the photo on the piano and a suppressed fantasy that I would grow up to resemble our mother. I didn't.

Much later my aunt occasionally took me to Cheltenham cemetery near Port Adelaide to see my mother's grave, but the cryptic headstone gave little away: 'In my Father's house'. People no longer tend graves and even then, in the mid-1950s, the ritual was weakening. It meant very little to me in adolescence. To me, being in Adelaide meant life, not death. It also meant that, like my mother, I was to have a career, as a teacher. Only recently, after my father's death in 1975 and in the light of feminist history, has the resonance of this remote set of events returned to me.

In certain sympathetic circumstances the role of the motherless child may be quite congenial. My earliest memories are of the happiest kind. At the onset of Edna Roe's fatal illness I was delivered 160 or so kilometres up-country to the household of my maternal grandmother,

Elizabeth Newman Heath, of Pygery. I remained there on her farm in the care of my mother's unmarried sister Isabella, called Isie, for the next four years. The household included young uncles, and I enjoyed a privileged position. Life among the Heaths, some of whom were settled on nearby farms with large families of their own, was my wheatlands version of *Childhood at Brindabella*.

My three sisters who remained home on the farm at Yallunda Flat had reason to believe I was spoilt by the years at Pygery. Isie Heath, who spent her whole life caring for others, the latter part in service in Adelaide, endured a lifetime's rough teasing as the family's 'unclaimed treasure'. She was a direct and capable countrywoman whose Christian faith sustained her to the end, and she did her best for me. Later I had cause to remember her well-cooked meals, my neat clothes and the handmade toys, not to mention constant attentions. On Fridays we would set off in Grandma's gleaming 1920s automobile for the shops of Wudinna, where Auntie Isie paraded the plump child along the dusty streets and kindly countrywomen extended the approval which it was all too easy to assume was one's natural due. We also went to the Church of England in Pygery Hall once a month, and to Pygery twice weekly for the mail in the buckboard. It was an ambiguous living arrangement though, and it ended abruptly, as Auntie Isie recalled, on 24 December 1945, when I was of school age and my father came to reclaim me.

Pygery was dry country, just inside Goyder's line, only lately productive due to superphosphate and the Tod River pipeline from the south, running in tandem with a rather extravagant narrow-gauge railway line which killed the many small ports of the peninsula. The two lines ran up the spine of the Peninsula, through sandy mallee which men from both sides of the family had helped to clear. My father, for example, though a modest man, would sometimes boast that he had cleared four scrub farms.

Truly, 'our father cleared the bush'. Or rather the mallee. It is sometimes said you can pick South Australians by their practice of pioneer worship, but it is relevant here that my forebears were pioneers, on one of the last small-farming frontiers. Although not obviously attractive country, there was life in the mallee and it could win hearts, as when topped by she-oaks or fringed with quandong. The Roes and the Heaths assumed themselves part of a people's history of Australia – a history, however, that excluded Aboriginal peoples, who had long since been rounded up on reserves and driven to fringe-dwelling despair in the earlier squatting age. For myself, I revelled in the mallee: it was child-sized, my first home, though in the years at Pygery I saw it mainly from the car or the front of my Uncle Doug's would-be racehorses. I was too small to play far beyond the pepper trees and the boobialla protecting the flat-roofed farmhouse from the north-west winds, which are the most unpleasant feature of the South Australian climate.

The idea that women have been undervalued in Australia came as a surprise to me at first. On South Australia's west coast, where the pioneering generation is only now dying out, women worked hard and were valued accordingly. My father, who got along well with women, maintained there were three categories: fine, sweet, and neurotic. Basically, 'neurotic' women were a nuisance in rural life, woe betide timid townies, the housebound, wastrels and worse. My forebears were certainly not neurotic. Both my grandmothers bore large families in the bush and ran farms long after their husbands'

John Roe and his daughters, Jean, Heather, myself and Pauline, taken at Port Lincoln on my return from Pygery in 1945.

deaths. Grandmother Heath was failing in health by my time, frail and painfully hunchbacked – a warning to stand up straight. Sometimes the Flying Doctor had to be called to her – an exciting event as the Bush Church Aid plane from the base at Ceduna touched down in the front paddock. After nearly 30 years on the frontier, Grandmother Heath remained a remarkably sweet person. Grandmother Roe, on the other hand, belonged to the 'fine woman' category. Though I hardly knew her – in any case, she disliked girls – it was obvious she was strong-minded and a more likely source of family prosperity than her long-departed husband, a horse-dealer. Having retired to Port Lincoln from the farm in the Cummins district, she amassed considerable town property, keeping a firm eye on her many sons, who benefited from her business acumen and held her in great respect. My grandfathers, like my mother, were an unknown quantity to me, a reminder, if any was needed, of the rigours and hazards on the frontier.

The different styles of grandmothers serve as rough symbol of my transition from Pygery to Yallunda Flat. Certainly things were very different, even the physical environment.

CHAPTER 1

Getting there

location – the first peoples – explorers – jetties and ports – the rail – cars, trucks and buses – by air – what lies ahead?

When I say I come from Eyre Peninsula, I am sometimes met with a blank look. This is hardly surprising since for many Australians, maybe most, it still seems rather remote, and I left there as a schoolgirl in the 1950s. In my time the south of the Peninsula was at least a day's drive from Adelaide, the nearest big city, and the boat trip took overnight, though the more recent option of air travel took little more time initially than it does now. Even so, it seems quicker to get there these days, and more people are aware of the region, having travelled across the northern edge to or from Perth – the Eyre Highway was finally bitumenised in 1973 – or been there as tourists, maybe to Coffin Bay, famous for its oysters. But it is still somewhat 'off the beaten track'. This opening chapter seeks to address two basic questions: where is Eyre Peninsula exactly, and what are the principal ways of getting there?

Location

Eyre Peninsula is situated about halfway across southern Australia. It is the largest of South Australia's three peninsulas, located some 200 kilometres to the west of Adelaide as the crow flies, and up to three times that distance by land via Port Augusta. Unusually for a peninsula, which dictionaries tell us are mostly areas of sea-bound land connected to the mainland by a narrow isthmus, it is shaped like an inverted triangle, with three sides of more or less equal length, and is contiguous with the State's interior. The northern boundary, which is not clearly defined, is land-based and runs west from Port Augusta to Ceduna or thereabouts. The two southward-extending sides are defined by sea, on the east by Spencer Gulf from its northernmost point at Port Augusta to the Port Lincoln area in the far south, and in the west by the Southern Ocean from beyond Ceduna down to Cape Catastrophe, a historic headland of some grandeur where the two sides converge. Altogether, the three boundaries encompass a landmass of some 70,000 square kilometres; this makes Eyre Peninsula the second largest peninsula in Australia after Cape York in Far North Queensland.

The First Peoples

In historical terms, Eyre Peninsula is one of the oldest parts of Australia. It predates even the ancient Gondwana landmass, from which it emerged at the south-eastern edge some four billion years ago. In that respect even the Aboriginal peoples who settled there as many as 50,000 years ago represent a blip in time, and European colonisation far less.

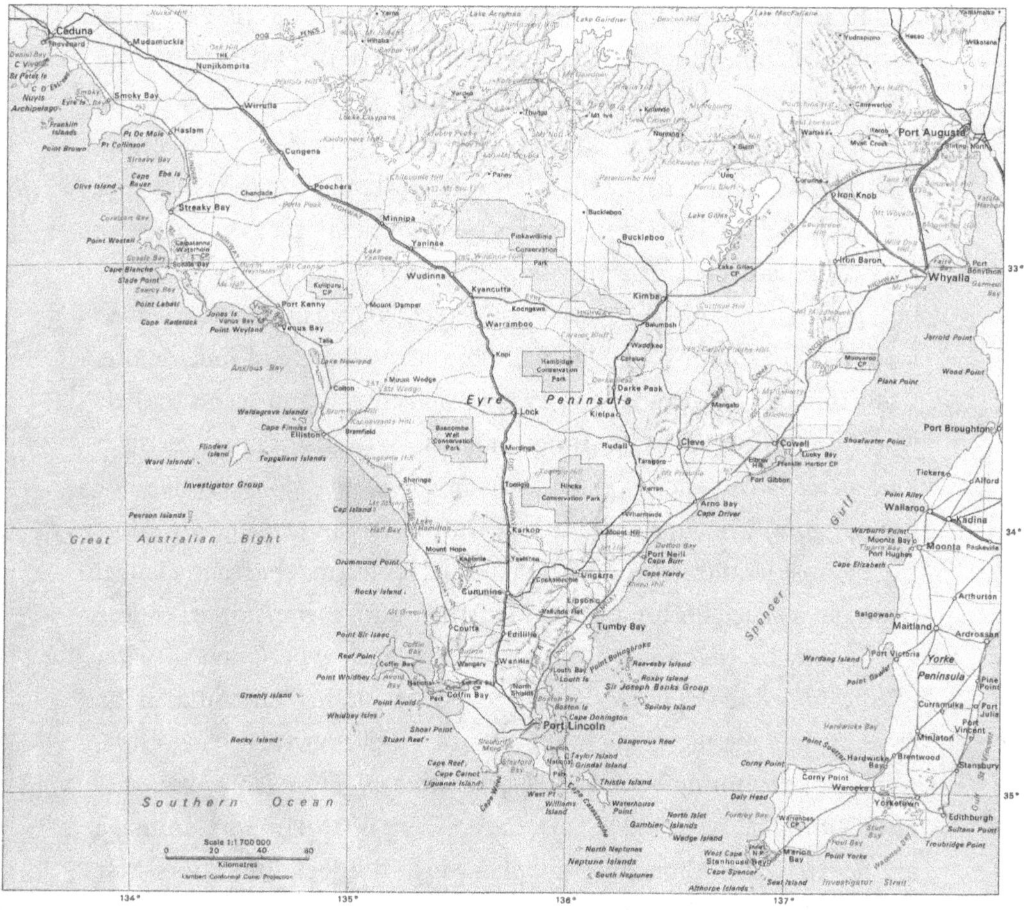

Map of Eyre Peninsula.

[Mapland, Department of Environment, Water and Natural Resources]

Exactly how and from where the three main groups of Aboriginal people on Eyre Peninsula at the time of European colonisation – the Banggarla in the north-east, the Wirangu in the north-west, and the Nawu to the south – came to be there remains a matter of conjecture, though it seems safe to say that they came by land from the north and that, although there were never very many of them, they occupied the region undisturbed for a very long time, surviving in the far-from-lush region as hunters and gatherers. Today they occupy some reserved lands west of Ceduna, and lay claim to the ownership of much more. Unfortunately, however, the story is a troubled one, and access to their world is a process difficult, if not impossible, to historicise over such long periods of time. Nonetheless some evidence does survive, for example the fish traps at the tip of Dutton Bay in the south-west of the Peninsula and it is now known that ochre traders from Central Australia reached Port Augusta and further south in pre-contact times.[1]

It may be that we will never know exactly when, and to what effect, Aboriginal peoples came to occupy Eyre Peninsula in its entirety, but the bigger picture casts some light on their way of life. In his prize-winning book *The Biggest Estate on Earth: How Aborigines made Australia*, published in 2011, the eminent historian Bill Gammage argues that the Aboriginal peoples were in effect Australia's first conservationists. By practising selective seasonal burning off, they maintained a balance between natural growth and their own needs as hunters and gatherers, and they ensured the ongoing health of the land itself. Even on remote Eyre Peninsula, where rainfall is for the most part limited, the early explorers would sometimes note the park-like effects that this approach encouraged. Certainly there is much still to be learned about this subject, but an acknowledgement of the prior

Fish traps near Dutton Bay. [Pat Green]

occupancy and enduring presence of the first peoples must come first in this chapter, as it seldom did for the incoming Europeans.

Explorers

For the European colonisers, the story would be very different. Apart from anything else, they came by sea, and we know much more about them. Although in my school days we didn't have many heroes, except perhaps some sportsmen, we did learn about the early explorers, both at school and from the popular culture. For us, there were two, maybe three, who really mattered.

First in our esteem was the meticulous Matthew Flinders, RN, who in the HMS *Investigator* in 1802 charted 'the unknown coast' of what was then New South Wales, from Fowlers Bay in the far west all

Monument to Matthew Flinders on Stamford Hill in 1912.
[SLSA PRG280/1/44/499]

the way east to what we now know to have been the mouth of the River Murray near Encounter Bay (so-called because that was where Flinders encountered French explorer Nicolas Baudin coming from the opposite direction). Flinders's wonderfully detailed charts, published in London in 1814 and since re-issued by the State Library of South Australia, are testimony to his skill and commitment.[2]

Close behind in our esteem was the intrepid Edward John Eyre, after whom the Peninsula was named by the governor of the new Colony of South Australia in 1839 (known at first as Eyre's Peninsula, and later simply Eyre Peninsula). It was Eyre who in 1839, aged 24, with overseer John Baxter and two Aboriginal companions, first traversed the west coast of the Peninsula by land, returning to Adelaide from

Eyre and Wylie pictured in *Eyre's Journey to Albany*, by Samuel Calvert, 1891.
[SLV IAN01/01/91/SUPP/12]

Streaky Bay via the Gawler Ranges and Lake Torrens. Despite having found that country unpromising, soon after he undertook what is described in the *Australian Dictionary of Biography* as an 'incredible journey' westward, from Port Lincoln along the Great Australian Bight to Albany. His only surviving Aboriginal companion was Wylie, who joined the expedition at Fowlers Bay.[3]

There was also the less widely known surveyor John Charles Darke, who in 1844 was fatally speared by a group of Aborigines at Waddikee Rocks up-country and buried under the peak that now bears his name. A memorial grave in the bush nearby is one of the few overt reminders of the clash between the Aboriginal peoples and the colonisers that occurred in the 1840s. Despite being few in number, the Aboriginal people of Eyre Peninsula are now said by historians to have put up the fiercest resistance to the European colonisation of South Australia.[4]

Had we known about Pieter Nuyts, we might have added him to the list. Nuyts was a Dutch mariner and the highest-ranking official aboard the Dutch East India Company vessel the *Gulden Seepaert* (*Golden Seahorse*), captained by Francors Thyssen. As far back as 1627, on company orders, the *Gulden Seepaert* explored the southern coast of New Holland/Australia from Cape Leeuwin on the south-western tip of the continent to the Nuyts Archipelago, so named subsequently by Flinders, on the western edge of Eyre Peninsula where Ceduna now sits. The journey not only produced the first reliable charts of the coastline from present-day Albany to Ceduna, but also the first European knowledge of what became South Australia. But it was not until the publication of a *Supplement* to the *Australian Dictionary of Biography* in 2005 that much was known about Nuyts, and in any event the credit really belongs to Thyssen and his crew.

Some of the later, lesser explorations by land, mostly undertaken by early pastoralists (a polite word for squatters), would certainly have appealed to us too. Despite being difficult of approach, the interior has always had its allure, the Gawler Ranges on the northern edge of the Peninsula in particular, at least to the more adventurous of us. It is fascinating to follow on from Eyre's trek across this semi-arid terrain of the Wirangu in 1839 to the 1857 expedition of Stephen Hack, whose family included some of the more colourful early settlers of South Australia. Hack found the area promising, with sufficient pasture and water to support pastoral leases, but a subsequent survey was far less favourable. Nonetheless some pastoral settlement did occur in the 1860s, for example at the still-operational Yardea Station, which soon after also became a post and telegraph station.[5] The later movement of settlers across Spencer Gulf to the area around Cowell as recorded by Frank Masters in *Saga of Wangaraleednie* also threw up some memorable characters. My farmer father thought this a fine book and encouraged me to read it.[6]

The school history book *Australia since 1606*, written by Professor Portus of the University of Adelaide, may have introduced us to other impressive characters, but it concentrated on the explorers of the north-west coast of Australia, such as William Dampier. Moreover, although we knew about the whalers and sealers who found their way from the north of Van Diemen's Land and Kangaroo Island to Eyre Peninsula in the early years of the 19th century, we weren't very impressed by them. A few traces remained – there were remnants of a shipwreck in the sand at Sleaford Bay in my day – but by all accounts the whalers were a rough lot. What we would have thought had we known that escaped convicts may have reached the islands off the coast prior to the establishment of the Province of South Australia in 1836, or that as early as the 1840s bushmen on the Peninsula were familiar with convict-derived slang, is now impossible to say.[7]

Jetties and ports

It could take well over a fortnight for the early colonists to reach Port Lincoln from Adelaide by land due to the necessity of rounding Spencer Gulf at Port Augusta, either by horse or on foot, and even by sea the journey might have taken several days. It must have been a relief to arrive at the tiny settlement but, on arrival by boat, people would at first have had to wade or be rowed ashore, or both, as the first jetty was not built until 1857, some 18 years after the first white settlers landed on the shores of Boston Bay. Still there, the Town Jetty, as it is now known, is located at the centre of the city and used mainly by fishermen and for recreation. The main jetty further down the bay at Kirton Point dates from 1906 and, along with related constructions, is now the main service point for shipping in southern Eyre Peninsula. With huge wheat silos attached, it dominates the cityscape.

Jetties have played an important role in the history of Eyre Peninsula. Between the 1860s and the 1920s, some 39 jetties were built along the Peninsula's estimated 3200 kilometres of coastline, from as far west as Fowlers Bay to Port Pirie on the eastern side of Spencer Gulf and on nearby islands. This may not sound a lot, but, as will be evident from a glance at a map of the peninsula, by the early 20th century the region was well served by coastal shipping – mainly ketches and schooners – and it should be remembered that some stretches of the coastline, especially the majestic limestone cliff faces of the west coast but also some of the sandy eastern bays, were not suited to jetty building, or necessitated the building of very long jetties, as at Port Germein – until recently the longest jetty in South Australia.[8] A telling instance of how tricky the approaches could be is the early pastoral port of Elliston, halfway up the west coast, where it was sometimes impossible for ships carrying essential supplies to enter Waterloo Bay, with its narrow entrance and uncertain tides. The misery that attended the turning back of ships is only too easily imagined.

Many older residents of Eyre Peninsula can recall when the arrival of 'the boat' was a main event of the week. At Tumby Bay, where I watched it most frequently, you had to be there at the right moment to see it come in. This meant on a Tuesday at about 2 pm, and thus for me in the early 1950s, during school holidays. There I'd be on the beach, with the small east-coast township at my back, squinting towards Port Lincoln, past the estuary of a mangrove-fringed creek and a then uninhabited rocky headland, hoping to see the Adelaide Steamship Company's MV *Morialta* appear on the horizon and watch it berth at the town's main jetty. There was something exciting about the way it suddenly bore down on you, and the Scottish-built ship had a certain style, due in part to a painted funnel.

There were always people on the jetty to welcome the *Morialta*, in addition to the wharfies busy loading and unloading cargo. Indeed, on most days you would find people scattered along the jetty, fishing, chatting, and otherwise relaxing. For them, as for many people living on Eyre Peninsula, jetties had become an integral part of life by the 1950s. The regular arrival of shipping at the small ports along the coast provided a focal point for town and country folk alike.

There were two jetties at Tumby Bay at that time. The older, shorter one, which was finally demolished in the 1990s, dated back to the 1870s, when it was built to serve various mining ventures in the hills to the west of the town, and it was still being used a century later for recreation and shade on hot days. It even had a diving board. The main jetty, a longer and stronger construct a few hundred metres to the south, dates from the early 1900s and thankfully still survives. Only just, however. In 1972 the body responsible for the state's jetties decided that Tumby's days as a port were over and, with costly maintenance needed on one section of the jetty, prepared to demolish it. When work was about to begin, appalled residents formed a picket line at the town end of the jetty, and the demolition was called off. Since then, with extra funding from local sources, the jetty has been strengthened and is as popular as ever. It features in all the town's advertising, and is part of its not inconsiderable tourist appeal.[9]

It is no wonder jetties were popular. They enlivened many small coastal settlements and, with many parts of the wheat-growing areas far from the coast, were a godsend to farmers. Prior to the building of jetties, farmers had had to get their grain harvest to the beaches by horse and cart, load it onto small boats and row the boats out to deeper water to be re-loaded onto the waiting ketches – when they turned up, that is. Even after the coming of rail, it was still cheaper in some places to use what was called the 'mosquito fleet' in the 1930s. (As a student at the University of Adelaide in the mid-1930s, the historian Russel Ward once worked on 'the mosquito fleet' during the long vacation.[10]) With the jetties in place, produce could be brought to storage sheds at the base of the jetty, sent on trolleys up the jetties and loaded straight into holds.

By now, however, the future of these historic constructs is far from secure because, as the story of the Tumby jetty may suggest, they are costly to maintain. In an attractive publication entitled *Jetties of South Australia: Past and present* published in 2005, compiler Neville Collins warns that ,while major bulk-handling ports such as Port Lincoln and Thevenard are flourishing, as maybe some recreational sites are also, the smaller jetties are under threat. Indeed, some have already gone, such as the jetty at the historic port of Lipson near Tumby, which was demolished as early as 1935. Collins does not spell it out, but it seems clear from his outline that the economic underpinning is slipping away and that there will need to be strong community support and a profitable tourist industry to sustain them.

It must have been some subliminal awareness of this situation that caused me to decide, on a journey back to the Peninsula in January 2007 as a preliminary to this project, that I would walk the surviving jetties. And, with a couple of regrettable omissions – of the tiny village of Haslam on Anxious Bay, south of Ceduna, of which I was unaware at the time, and Port Neill, north of Tumby Bay, where I missed the turnoff – I more or less did just that: from Fowlers Bay, baking in the hot sun way out west, to as far as the fish nets piled up on the Cowell jetty at Franklin Harbour, halfway up Spencer Gulf. Admittedly I was not brave enough to walk the entire length of the narrow jetty at Elliston on a chilly Sunday morning by myself, and it seemed enough at the time to find that the now somewhat shortened jetty at the lovely but solitary Louth Bay was still there, but overall it was an enriching experience, and one to be recommended to visitors.

Perhaps it was on one of the jetties fronting Spencer Gulf that I was reminded of the once-ubiquitous advertising slogan, accompanied by the ringing of ships' bells, 'It's time YOU went on the Gulf Trip'. Introduced before World War I by one of the three shipping companies then competing for the coastal trade, the Gulf Trip became a standby of the Adelaide Steamship Company, which had gained a monopoly on the coastal trade by 1915, and proved popular in the interwar years. There were two main variants on offer: a short trip from Port Adelaide to Port Lincoln with a brief stay there (three to four days), and a longer trip from Port Adelaide to Port Augusta with calls at Port Lincoln, Cowell, Whyalla, Port Pirie and the old copper port of Wallaroo (six days).[11] Travel up the west coast was never such an enticing prospect, with long stretches of towering cliffs and some dangerous bays along the way. The most worrisome was surely Elliston, where bad weather and rough seas meant shipwrecks sometimes occurred. Safer harbours further west, at Ceduna in Denial Bay for instance, made things easier, but these remote and not especially productive parts had their own problems. There was even an occasional mishap in the normally placid waters off Tumby Bay, and the waters near 'the Althorpes' between Kangaroo Island and the western tip of Yorke Peninsula had a reputation for roughness.[12]

It may sound as if the maritime history of Eyre Peninsula is an uncertain story, for all its variety and interest. It was undoubtedly rough-and-ready at times, and it is true that its most colourful aspect – the great grain races that saw mighty sailing ships arrive in Spencer Gulf from Europe until as late as 1949 – was already becoming a thing of the past by the onset of World War II.[13] But local and coastal shipping still seemed sound after the war, with several larger passenger/cargo ships in operation in the 1950s. MV *Moonta*, built in Denmark in 1931, lasted until 1955, when its cargo side became unprofitable and it was sold off; it had offered six-day trips from Port Adelaide to Port Augusta and back which took in Kangaroo Island. It ended up being used as a casino on a beach on the South Coast of France. The *Morialta*, purpose-built pre-war but not brought into service until after World War II, lasted only a year longer, until 1956; a comfortable ship, it was advertising cruises to the smaller ports of the lower Gulf, from Adelaide to Cowell and back via Tumby Bay, Port Neill and Arno Bay in 1950. Three years later, in 1960, the queen of them all, the MV *Minnipa* – another Danish-built ship which began its 33-year service to Eyre Peninsula in 1927 – was finally withdrawn from service, due to a decline in patronage. With that, the coastal shipping that dated back to 1839 seemed to come to an end.

It was not quite the end, however. Kangaroo Island could not do without shipping entirely. Nor, as it turned out, could Eyre Peninsula. After some protracted manoeuvres, the *Troubridge*, a state-owned 'ro-ro' (roll-on, roll-off) service to Port Lincoln was finally in place by the early 1970s and, more recently, a privately operated 'ro-ro' service was introduced between Wallaroo and Lucky Bay, north of Cowell, which cuts off hours of travel by road to Adelaide. As well, Thevenard in the west and the recently constructed Port Bonython north of Whyalla are essential outlets for the mining industries, and a deepwater port to serve possible iron ore projects along the east and centre of the Peninsula is projected for the otherwise unprepossessing Sheep Hill north of Tumby Bay and two other sites nearby. Long jetties will surely be needed there, like the one built at Port Bonython – now the longest jetty in South Australia (see note 7 for details).

There was always something more to the coming and going of shipping to the Peninsula in times past: the mail. The early shipping companies competed for the contracts to carry the mail and, chaotic as it may have been at times, thus provided another vital service. A delightful little book on South Australia's postal history produced by Australia Post for South Australia's sesquicentenary in 1986, entitled *The Personal Touch*, says that when it came to postal services from Ceduna to Whyalla 'everything depended on coastal shipping' (p. 15).

Elsewhere in Australia the mail was increasingly delivered by road or rail, and these days it comes by plane, but on Eyre Peninsula until well into the 20th century there were parts of the interior where delivery remained problematic, a matter of smaller contractors working out from the ports by road. This was the case for us at Yallunda Flat in the 1950s. We were a mere 50 or so kilometres inland from Port

The Overland Mail, Port Lincoln to Eucla, 1881–1890.
[*The Personal Touch*]

Lincoln, but tucked away in the hills, and a proposed rail link from Cummins to Tumby Bay that would have passed through was never actually built. Thus the mail (and fresh bread) was delivered twice weekly by bus from Port Lincoln to the Yallunda Flat general store, leaving us to collect it (sometimes by me on horseback – how much of the high-top loaves made it home on those occasions is another question . . .).

The Personal Touch contains a far more dramatic illustration of the difficulties faced by the postal service in remote parts with a photograph of a mail contractor in horse and cart making his way along a rough track westward from Port Lincoln to Eucla in the 1880s. The booklet also contains a telling photograph from the 1920s of the mail arriving by rail at a recently built siding called Pygery up beyond Wudinna, which again I once knew well. It is a reminder of how far the

The mail train departing Pygery, 1929.
[*The Personal Touch*]

mail and the mailmen had to go to ensure delivery of the many letters which were until quite recently the main way people kept in touch with family and friends. It may be noted in passing that those same local distribution points usually housed telephone exchanges too, the last of which, at north-west Mudamuckla (what a wonderful name: from the Aboriginal, it is said to mean 'sore knee', 'water supply' or maybe 'sea fish'), closed as recently as 1987.[14]

In 'Pleasure and Nostalgia', the final chapter of his book *Southern Passages: A maritime history of South Australia*, historian Ronald Parsons notes that little now remains of the earlier modes of communication by sea outside of specialist collections in libraries, except the surviving jetties and remnants of shipwrecks. To the preservation of knowledge about that lost world, Eyre Peninsula has made at least one significant contribution: the Axel Stenross Museum at Port Lincoln. Stenross was a Finnish sailor who signed off from one of the great grain ships at

Port Lincoln in 1927 and remained to work as a boat builder until 1939, when he took over a slip at Happy Valley at the northern end of the city and ran a ship-building and repair yard there for the rest of his life.

Stenross's slip was one of the first – and rather mysterious – sights my sisters and I would see coming into Port Lincoln from the north. These days the museum established by locals in his memory flourishes as a tourist attraction. It offers a working representation of traditional shipbuilding and contains a large collection of materials about the slip.

More recently I have learned a little more about the numerous lighthouses built around the coast and at the mouth of Spencer Gulf, mostly between the 1860s and the 1920s, to protect coastal shipping. Most of them have since been closed or superseded by other navigational aids, for which the Commonwealth became responsible as far back as 1915 (except for Point Lowly, north of Whyalla, where the city assumed responsibility in 1995). But we still felt anxious about passing through 'the Althorpes' at night when coming home from Adelaide by sea in the 1950s, despite a long-established lighthouse there, and shipwrecks cannot be entirely avoided.[15]

The rail

On Eyre Peninsula as elsewhere, but maybe more obviously there, shipping and railways have long been interrelated, with Port Lincoln in the south and Ceduna/Thevenard in the west the main terminals for both shipping and the railways to the present day.

Compared with shipping, the coming of the rail to Eyre Peninsula is a recent development. The building of railways dates from 1906, when legislation in the State Parliament authorised work to begin on the construction of a railway to promote closer settlement and agriculture, especially the growing of wheat, in the hitherto undeveloped interior of the Peninsula. The resultant system runs on narrow gauge (known colloquially as the three foot six gauge) and is a stand-alone network, with no connection to the state's mainland system or with the India–Pacific line from Sydney to Perth, despite a potentially linking line from Whyalla to Port Augusta which opened in 1975 but runs on a different (standard) gauge.

As outlined by Peter Knife in his informative account entitled *Peninsula Pioneer: A history of the railways of Eyre Peninsula and their role in the early settlement and development of the region* (2006), the railway was built in three main stages and reached its fullest extent in the 1950s. As is so often the case with transport history, a map tells the story most succinctly. It shows that at that time the main line ran up the hinterland from Port Lincoln to Ceduna/Thevenard, with several branch lines – from Yeelanna to Mount Hope in the south-west, from Cummins to Kimba and Buckleboo in the north-east, and from Ceduna to Penong in the far west. (There was also a stand-alone private line run by BHP between Iron Knob and Whyalla in the north-east dating from 1900.) Later, however, when numerous sidings were closed and some branch lines were closed altogether, two new ones were built: the line to Whyalla from Port Augusta, and another from the gypsum field at Kevin, south of Penong, to connect with the main line at Ceduna.

It was customary when opening a new line to offer the locals a free ride. Grainy photographs of large open trucks filled with cheering youngsters testify that this was done when railway building first got going at Port Lincoln and again when the main line reached Cummins, 42 kilometres inland to the north. That historic day in

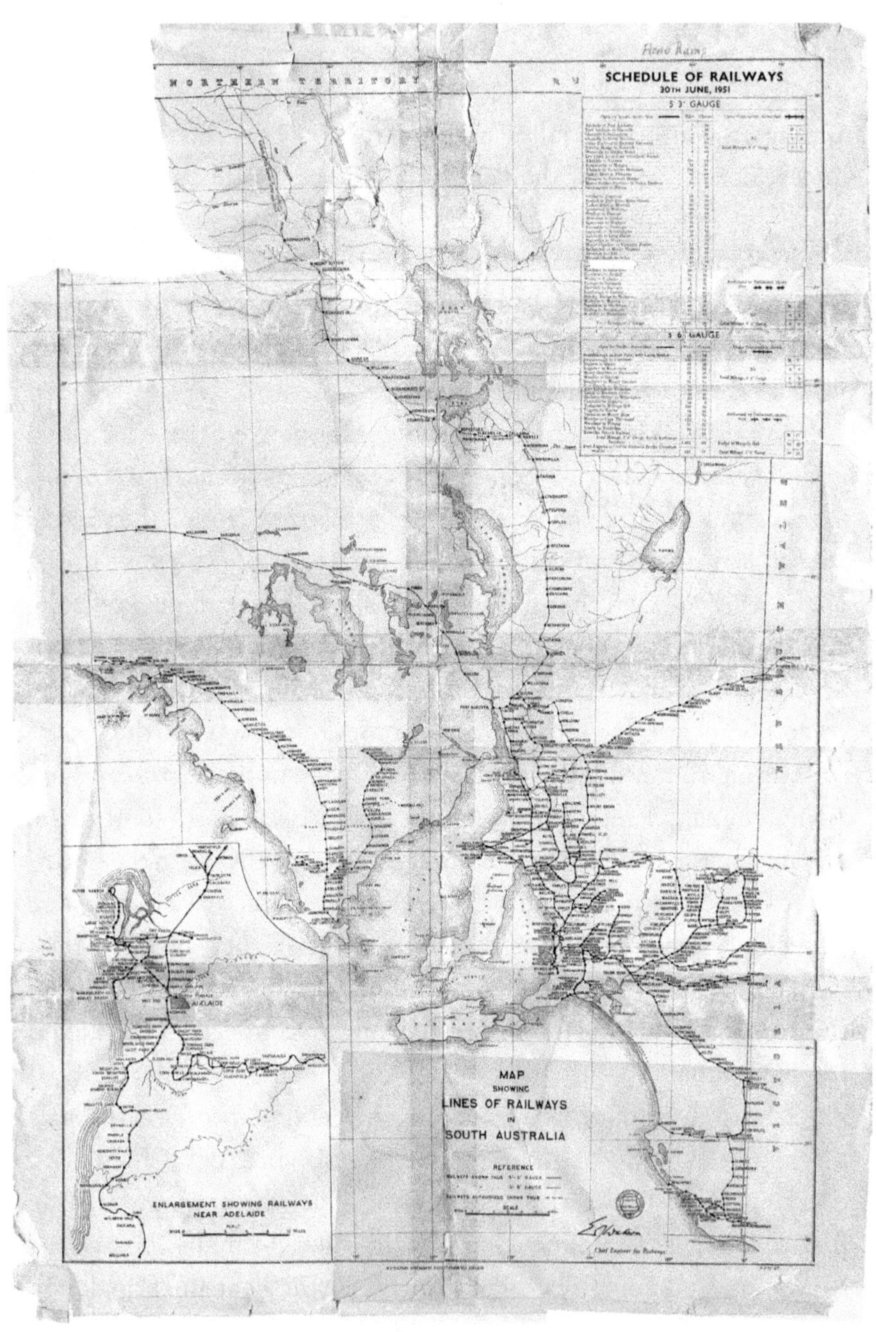

1956 map of South Australian railways.

[National Railway Museum]

November 1907 is recorded in my grandmother Anna Roe's diary. It was not long since the Roes had travelled by sea from Yorke Peninsula to Tumby Bay and then cross-country to take up land at Marble View to the south-east of Cummins. Anna Roe writes in her matter-of-fact way that the family went down to the newly built line to catch a glimpse of the passing cavalcade.

Reaching Cummins and then a short way beyond Yeelanna in 1909, marked completion of the first stage of railway construction. The next and most extensive phase followed a Royal Commission in 1911–1913 on the future development of railways in the region. The land still to be opened up to agriculture lay well to the north of Cummins and a railway was needed to facilitate that. With a large gang of navvies arriving at Port Lincoln in early 1912, as they had in 1906, work began almost immediately. The only contentious issue was where the line would end. The Commissioners had recommended Decres Bay south of Ceduna, but Thevenard was found to be cheaper and safer so that was that. A line to Thevenard was finished in early 1915.

It was to this interior that my maternal grandfather, Thomas Robert Heath, and his oldest son, Roy, went from Warratta Vale near Lipson to inspect a block of land at Pygery in 1915. The block remained in the Heath family until the 1990s, and there are still Heath relatives at Kyancutta, but unfortunately both Roy and his father died shortly after arrival up-country, Roy from influenza, and the Heath family was not able to settle on the land until 1919. Some younger Roes went up the country at much the same time, and stayed almost as long as the Heaths. Other hopefuls came to the area cross-country via Cowell and Port Augusta, but the rail from Port Lincoln to Ceduna/Thevenard was always the main conduit.

At 434 kilometres the main line to Ceduna/Thevenard was by far the longest line built during the second phase of railway building on Eyre Peninsula, but it was not the only one of what Knife has called the 'Royal Commission' lines. A substantial side line was built to the north-east from Cummins to Darke Peak and on to Kimba between 1912 and 1913, and a year later a smaller one, west from Yeelanna to Mount Hope, almost to the coast, the building of which, like so many early country branch lines in Australia, owed its existence more to politics than economics. Interestingly, to me at least, Cummins would become a hub of the system, and also the site of regional cattle and sheep sales until about 1960. How well I remember the stockyards across the road from my grade nine classroom at Cummins Area School and hearing the auctions being conducted there, weekly if I recall correctly.

A third building phase consisted of minor extensions in the 1920s, one being from Kimba to Buckleboo, a major grain collection point

A passenger carriage of the 1940s. [Port Lincoln Railway Museum]

at the margins of northern cultivation, which, when I saw it in 2007, consisted of numerous huge silos and what was probably a staff house, protected by a fearsome dog. Another extension was built off the Ceduna–Penong line, the previously mentioned gypsum line to Kevin.

I can still remember the train trip from Cummins to Pygery and back in the late 1940s. It took about three hours and we passed through one small township and siding after another, many of them with exotic names based on Aboriginal words, such as Karkoo (said to be Aboriginal for she-oak) and Kopi (said to be Aboriginal for gypsum). Even at an early age I usually travelled alone. At Cummins station, my recently widowed father left me in the care of the guard of the single carriage that went up the line twice weekly, and at Pygery siding I was met by a male relative who collected the mail and took me to stay with my grandmother and my mother's sister.

These days the main function of the railway is the transportation of wheat and other grains to port. The trains no longer carry passengers, and whereas even quite small stations once had refreshment rooms, these are not provided or indeed needed these days. Nowadays silos are the main buildings. I vividly recall seeing farmers and their grain-loaded trucks lined up at Poochera when pausing there for lunch in January 2007. Fortunately I'd brought my own.

When discussing railway history, people sometimes get stuck at the trains and the rails. This is understandable, but far from the whole story. There is more to it than economics, basic as that aspect is: as Peter Knife puts it in the conclusion to his *Peninsula Pioneer*, Eyre Peninsula would not be the economic success it is today without the fundamental role played by the railways in opening up the inland for agriculture. However, as Knife also points out, the only towns there before the coming of rail were Port Lincoln, Ceduna and Penong. That is to say, there was a social dimension to the building of railways through the interior. It was not just that little girls like me could once travel up and down the lines in safety, or even that, as I can just remember, the rail brought my youngest uncle safe home from World War II; it was also that the railways helped build communities in the new lands. As well as the planning of lines and placement of sidings, sites for towns and townships were surveyed along the lines. Being South Australia, a 'parklands model' was sometimes used, and in one or two places plans were drawn up for a garden suburb-type township, difficult as it now is to imagine this at Thevenard or Karcultaby.[16]

The railways brought people to these places, first the railway workers, then shopkeepers and the like. Given that many of the navvies were immigrants (and in later years European immigrants), they added social diversity and, on their weekends off, vitality to the towns. Later, when the lines were fully operational, they required regular maintenance workers. So it was that railway workers and their families were to be found in most if not all of the small towns and townships along the main lines. Happily their experiences have not gone un-recorded. In an oral history entitled *Rail on Eyre* (2001), compiler Alice Domagalski of Edillilie has gathered the diverse memories of railway workers and their families. This includes English migrant Elsie Kirkham's 'Over the Hill and Around the Next Corner', which recalls starting out in one of three railway cottages at Tooligie, and Sylvia Laube's memories of water trucks on trains. More recently Kenneth and Margaret Knife have published another valuable work, *Peninsula Memories: Stories of the railwaymen and women of Eyre Peninsula* (2007).

Cars, trucks and buses

By the 1920s the worst problems of distance were probably over, but Eyre Peninsula was always remote, and it is no wonder that alternative modes of transport and communication were welcome. Change, when it came, came quickly. A photograph survives of a Roe uncle as a young man dressed in his best clothes standing by a brand new motorcar in the Mallee in the 1920s, probably at Pinkawillinie near Kimba. I cannot remember a time when my father did not have a motor vehicle of some kind: in the late 1940s a Ford utility, in the 1950s a black Dodge sedan and an old truck of indeterminate make, and from the 1960s a large and rather unworldly looking Valiant. Most country people believed, and rightly so, that American cars were stronger and better suited to the mostly execrable dirt roads than British cars. My maternal grandmother at Pygery had two motor vehicles by the 1940s: a 1920s silver sedan for trips to 'town' and special occasions ('Grandma's car'), and a battered utility for day-to-day use. Most if not all of the farming families had motor vehicles of some kind by the mid-20th century. Moreover many of the women could drive them, and some quite young people too. I learned myself at about age 13, taught by my father on the way home from church, when the roads were practically deserted.

Family cars were not the only new mode of transport dating from the 1920s. The 1920s also saw the beginnings of long distance road transport. For the young Ray Gilleland, who drove the big trucks right across the continent, passing through Port Augusta cross-country to Ceduna, they represented romance and adventure, as he records in his recent memoir *The Nullarbor Kid: Stories of my trucking life* (2012). When asked as a boy what he wanted to do, he said 'Just drive, you know just

Uncle Bill Roe (second from left) with friends and the first Roe car in 1924.

chase the horizon' (p. 19). A noticeable feature of his recall is how he felt himself to be in competition with the railways – as long-distance road transport was, though not along his coastal route. By the 1960s the bulk of goods from the peninsula, apart from grains and minerals, were moved by road transport, and most residents travelled by car and air. A study undertaken in the 1970s concluded that by then the region was well served by modern transport systems.

So too petrol was increasingly moved by road. Until the late 1950s it came up-country by rail from Port Lincoln, to be sold from bowsers outside the local garage or general store. Thereafter it would be delivered to purpose-built service stations by road tankers. The coming of service stations to rural Australia seems to be a subject in waiting. A nicely illustrated book entitled *Great Australian Service Stations* by

Jim Souter was published in 2011, but the only examples from South Australia appear to come from south of Adelaide and the lower Murray.

As for the state of the roads, almost entirely dirt until the later 20th century, it was a constant source of complaint. Local councils could barely keep up, and there are still plenty of 'Roads to Recovery' signs to be seen, especially in the north. Prior to the coming of rail and the car, the roads served a diverse clientele, including shearers on bikes, circus operators, and even occasionally gypsies. These days the main roads get heavy use from locals and tourists alike, and from every imaginable mode of transport.[17]

No account of road transport on Eyre Peninsula would be complete without the legendary bus driver Mrs Sylvia Birdseye, who for over 30 years drove a passenger and freight bus from Adelaide, first to Port Lincoln and later, on to Streaky Bay. Like many others, I remember her well, and there is no shortage of material on her.[18] One of the great characters of Peninsula history, she was born in the bush near Port Augusta in 1902, and by age 21 was in Adelaide working for Alfred Birdseye, who established South Australia's first motorised bus service. At first she drove buses to Mannum and then, having married into the Birdseye family and borne two children, to Port Augusta and thereafter on to Eyre Peninsula.

Mrs Birdseye, 1959.
[News Ltd / Newspix]

A Birdseye's Bus from Port Lincoln to Adelaide.

[John Masterton Collection]

It was said that in later years Mrs Birdseye drove 3000 kilometres a week. She was single-minded, intrepid, a competent mechanic, and did not suffer fools gladly. Many will recall that she was the first woman they had ever seen wearing trousers (she also wore jodhpurs). When she died, the *Port Lincoln Times* said she had been 'one of the most colourful and toughest little women in the State'. For a small woman, she seemed remarkably strong, single-handedly loading passengers' luggage on to the top of the bus, and keeping the buses on the road during the most difficult circumstances. After her husband died in 1954 she kept on driving, right up to her unexpected death in 1962, and her daughter maintained the business until 1980. Mrs Birdseye was buried at Goodwood in Adelaide and a memorial cairn can be seen on the

Eyre Highway near the Iron Knob turn off. The cross-country highway between Cowell and Elliston has also been named after her.

As a young person I regarded Mrs Birdseye with something like awe. Present-day long-distance bus services run along similar routes to those she drove, and in retrospect she was probably the nearest thing to a liberated woman we ever encountered.[19]

By air

The passing of Mrs Birdseye in 1962 serves as a turning point in the problem of reaching Eyre Peninsula and its interior. The end of passenger services on the railways in the late 1950s and the last *Minnipa* sailing in 1960 mark a time of transition in transport and communications. Except for the moving of heavy goods, which remains the domain of shipping and the railway, by the 1960s most things would go by road or air. With better roads and cars, it now takes less than seven hours to drive to Adelaide from Port Lincoln via Port Augusta, but it takes under an hour – 45 minutes or thereabouts – to fly from Port Lincoln to Adelaide airport. When last I did the trip, I sat next to a woman from Tumby Bay who was flying to Adelaide for the day to see a specialist.

When that remarkable polymath Robert Bedford was promoting air travel (and a separate state) for Eyre Peninsula in the 1930s, aeroplanes were still a new idea, even for country people, who immediately saw the advantage.[20] But it was not long before entrepreneurs of the air were setting up regional services everywhere, including on Eyre Peninsula. My earliest recollection is of Guinea Airlines, a company that originated in 1920s New Guinea and lasted until 1959, when it was taken over by Ansett.

Later I would occasionally experience the Ansett subsidiary Airlines of South Australia (ASA) Mark I, which provided an extensive service to the main towns of Eyre Peninsula between 1959 and 1986, and thereafter a service that continued, more or less, until 2005, when ASA Mark II operated independently of Ansett.

It seems that even before the demise of ASA, a new regional service was under way: Rex Airlines in Sydney. Established by ex-Qantas workers as an independent service, it now flies throughout the southern states of Australia as far as Eyre Peninsula and into Queensland. Qantas has also entered the fray with Qantaslink. The best part of these flights, apart from the brief length of time spent in the air, is the direct route over flat-as-a-board Yorke Peninsula. Sometimes you even fly over the dreaded Althorpes.

What lies ahead?

As the previously mentioned study of the Peninsula's transport systems undertaken in the 1970s concluded, by then the region was well served. In short 'getting there' was no longer a problem. By the late 20th century, when bulk-handling wharves had replaced jetties, trucks brought in the petrol, the mail arrived by plane and bus, and email was on its way, country people could rely on up-to-date modes of transport and, to a lesser extent, modern means of communication. So what lies ahead? How Eyre Peninsula will fare in a world increasingly dominated by broadband and the internet is another question. So too is the price of petrol.

CHAPTER 2

Country life

approaches – a trip in 2007 – museums – Koppio – closer settlement – from the 1920s – women and men – a turning point?

Approaches

In the summer of 2007 my friend and colleague the late Helen Bartley and I went back to Eyre Peninsula. Helen, a psychologist whose life began up-country near Wudinna, wanted especially to revisit that part. Her father, the only one of four enlisted men in her immediate family to survive World War I, went there as a soldier settler in the 1920s. I wanted to see the far west coast, much of it for the first time, and to gain a better feel for country life as it is today.

For many South Australians, 'country life' has always meant 'the good life'. However, by now a far smaller proportion of the state's population actually live in the country than a century ago and these days 'the good life' is more likely to mean life in the city. By the 1980s, according to Canberra political scientist Don Aitkin, 'country mindedness' was no more.[1]

While this may be so for some other parts of Australia, it hardly applies to Eyre Peninsula. There at the close of the 20th century most farms were still family farms and the land itself is more productive than ever. Moreover as Aitkin has more recently pointed out, there have been many new recruits to country living, not only retirees seeking a quiet life, but also people associated with new industries such as tourism and commercial fishing. Nor have country people been totally passive in the face of socio-economic change. In fact, as often as not, they have welcomed it, even mining, and these days they are increasingly laying claim to their own histories.[2]

By 2007 three decades had passed since I last set foot on Eyre Peninsula, apart from one short trip to attend the Yallunda Flat Show, and during that time much changed in standard approaches to country life. Some of the classic works of South Australian history have dealt with the rural experience, however most were written before historians discovered 'the other side of the frontier' in the 1980s, and things have never been quite the same since. European settlement, pastoralism, and agriculture have all tended to fall into disrepute.[3]

A second reason for taking a fresh look at country life is only now coming into view, that is, mining on prime agricultural land. This is currently a big and worrisome story in Queensland, and a fraught one in New South Wales, where the Liverpool Plains and further out the iconic Pilliga Scrub are under serious threat. So too apparently is much of eastern Eyre Peninsula.[4]

The third reason is harder to pin down, but it too matters, maybe even more. The relationship between the cities and country is now quite disproportionate in Australia, due to the economic rationalism of the 1980s, which meant the country was left to fend for itself, even though its wellbeing affects us all. As political scientist Judith Brett put it in a *Quarterly Essay* entitled 'Fair Share: Country and city in Australia', it is time to bring the country back in.[5]

A trip in 2007

Woodie – as she was always called – and I began our trip back to the Peninsula in 2007 by taking the car ferry across Spencer Gulf, from Wallaroo to Lucky Bay near Cowell. From Cowell, an old stone town with a comparatively long settler history and about a thousand residents, we went cross-country, through Cleve to Rudall, taking care to locate the memorial to children's writer May Gibbs along the way. At Rudall we turned north to see the memorial to explorer John Charles Darke, fatally speared by Aborigines in 1844, and next on through Kimba to Buckleboo, well beyond surveyor George Goyder's famous line, drawn by him in 1865 along approximately the 10-inch rainfall isohyet (c. 250 mm p.a.). It was at Buckleboo, which nowadays is little more than the end of a branch line, that we first saw a stand of the enormous wheat silos that have replaced the old sheds and stacks at the

Silos at Buckleboo, 2007.

The Big Galah at Kimba. [Our Naked Australia]

railway sidings of the interior. They made me realise how far north the rural frontier had moved in the 20th century and wonder what country people might be thinking about climate change. A recent biography of Goyder shows that the limits of arable land have varied over time.[6]

It was reassuring to get back to Kimba – once quite remote, now flourishing as an administrative centre and a stopover on the Eyre Highway, with a population approaching 700 at the 2011 census. Its big galah symbol sits up-front and there were masses of Sturt's Desert Pea in flower outside the main service station. Next day it was north-west, to Wudinna, passing through Kyancutta and its museum. The Wudinna area too is flourishing despite the now limited rail service, due, like Kimba, to the east–west road traffic, and to rural consolidation. Not that it is a big place even now, with some 1600 people living in and around the town at census time. Here I began to wonder if the actual pivot of Peninsula life had moved north. In retrospect, I recall not so much the summer stubble, of which there was plenty, but the proximity of the Gawler Ranges as a tourist attraction. This is not quite the hard country often envisaged, though it was hot and hard enough for me at the time.

It gets harder – and hotter – further up the highway, which follows the rail to Ceduna, and there was both less and more to take in. The familiar 'Roads to Recovery' signs seemed increasingly wishful, especially on the dirt road into what little remains of Nunjikompita. As for Mudamuckla, which I was looking forward to seeing, there is not much left there either. Less than one hundred people now live at the nearest port of Haslam, but they have managed to save some of its jetty, erected in 1911–1912. The Dutch almost reached this spot nearly four centuries ago.[7]

Inevitably the Stuart case comes to mind at Ceduna. I was a student at the University of Adelaide when Ken Inglis published his book on the subject in 1961, and we went out to Thevenard to look at the site. I also re-read the book (and saw the 2002 film *Black and White*) and tried to take in this perspective on the history of Eyre Peninsula. It is not easy, but you have to try. It is impossible to spend any time in Ceduna and beyond without noticing some aspect of race relations. Here too, in another guise, is the frontier – the racial frontier. However, there is now a substantial open-air museum on the edge of town, which encompasses many aspects of the area's experience. Altogether the official population of Ceduna and the contiguous port of Thevenard was 2649 in 2011, but if the transient Aboriginal population is included, 3000 seems more accurate.[8]

Turning south, for me there were two 'must sees' at Streaky Bay, a pleasing town with a population of over 1600 persons: St Augustine's Anglican Church, where the father of eminent Australian historian Frank Crowley was once rural dean, and the still rather grand Streaky Bay Community Hotel (previously Flinders Hotel), where Daisy Bates first stayed when she left hospital in Adelaide in 1945 'to be with my natives'. It may sound somewhat fanciful, but walking the Streaky Bay jetty it felt as if she was still there, in her starched collar and long black skirt, setting us all right. St Augustine's, unlike some other churches on the Peninsula, is still there, a handsome brick and stone building said to be an outstanding example of some 30-odd churches designed for the Diocese of Willochra by Port Pirie layman and banker William Kingsland Mallyon.[9]

Lest this approach seems somewhat self-indulgent, it is meant to convey something of the spirit of place and to touch lightly upon some aspects of country life as it appears these days. For more, we must move further down the coast, passing all too quickly by its grand coastline and its conflicted pastoral history. I had, of course, been following the historical research on the Elliston massacre, if that is the right phrase, and went to check out the site. When I saw the graduated cave-ridden cliffs there, it seemed to me that without more evidence of the conflict over land and its extent, the issues must remain unresolved. What did reassure at Elliston were the remains of the latest biennial cliff-top sculpture exhibition on the north side of the bay, and meeting some local sculptors subsequently. Was this tiny old town really Eyre Peninsula today?, I asked myself. Perhaps there has always been something special about Elliston, since Ellen Liston, one of South Australia's earliest writers, wrote pioneer tales here. In

The Elliston cliffs, 2007.

any event, the 'cultural turn' it represents is something to be taken into account.[10]

Finally, en route to Port Lincoln we called at Dutton Bay, where another interesting museum in an old stone woolshed presented itself, but we did not stop at Coffin Bay, possibly the best-known site of all those mentioned thanks to the famous Coffin Bay oysters. I had been to Coffins – as we always called it – many times when young and seen the site of the old Mortlock Station homestead, then on the outskirts of town. The fishing industry flourishes there, and it is a prime example of suburbanised holiday-making. Eyre Peninsula becomes a top tourist destination? By all means. So long as food production is sustained, surely.[11]

Speaking of tourism, travelling back up the eastern coast on the way back to Lucky Bay, we called at Tumby Bay, where I was born. It too has a Mallyon-designed Anglican church, St Margaret's, built on land donated by the Mortlocks and now over 100 years old. It is still a small town, with a population of some 1800, at first sight not much changed. Imagine my astonishment then when that summer's day it dawned on me that Tumby Bay is also now a tourist destination, maybe the Riviera of Eyre Peninsula. Writer Kate Llewellyn has recently sung its praises in her memoir *The Dressmaker's Daughter* (2008). If hematite mining goes ahead nearby, as seems quite likely, it will be even more changed.[12]

Museums

With tourism now a well-established industry on Eyre Peninsula, the museums have become fixed points on the tourist trail. Evidently the locals are more history-minded than in my day, when it was largely a matter of 'back to' events with the oldies out in period costume. As professional historian Geoffrey Speirs reminds us, interest in Australian history has burgeoned since the 1960s, and these days local history museums are to be found in many towns and suburbs, as well as an array of specialist museums established in the wake of the heritage movement, most of them maintained on a voluntary basis and established quite recently.[13]

The first and certainly the most unusual museum we saw was the Kyancutta Museum. Its founder was the previously mentioned Robert Bedford, a scientist and local entrepreneur, who emigrated from England at the onset of World War I and in 1915 took up land in this still remote place to grow wheat. A man of many talents, at Kyancutta

Bedford established, among other things, a cottage hospital, a radio station and an air service, and in 1924 a Museum of Evolution for the geological and anthropological specimens he collected on trips inland. The building and a post office are still there, but not his collection, which was dispersed after he died in 1951. Bedford was much admired throughout the region, though not at the museum in Adelaide, and thoroughly deserves the entry on him in the *Australian Dictionary of Biography*. Apart from anything else, like many early arrivals in rural and regional Australia, he cannot be stereotyped.[14]

The Ceduna museum is something else – a community in miniature, with numerous recreated historical buildings arranged around a large rectangle. For me its most compelling buildings were a tiny windowless lock-up and an old school room. There was a welcome domestic life dimension to the place too; unlike some country collections, the Ceduna museum is not dominated by farm machinery. But then farming is not such a big deal up there.

These days it seems all the towns along the west coast have local museums. Thus, as its website states, the Streaky Bay museum reflects farming activities prior to the late 1940s, with early agricultural and related machinery on display; the museum at Elliston has a 2005 bushfire display, and a somewhat perfunctory acknowledgement of a prior Aboriginal presence as part of a larger mural which makes it one of the few to attract wider attention; and further south there's the still functional woolshed museum at Dutton Bay.[15]

Koppio

Situated amid farmland in the picturesque Koppio Hills some 40 kilometres north of Port Lincoln, the Koppio museum is also a miniature historical community. There you can inspect Koppio's one-teacher school, one of the longest surviving such schools in the state (it closed in 1970), the old Whites Flat post office (said to be one of the smallest in the state), a Bank of Adelaide building, and more. As well, a number of display sheds house enough farm machinery and other equipment to satisfy busloads of schoolchildren.

There are several thought-provoking features to the Koppio museum or, more correctly, the 'Koppio Smithy Museum'. That is because it is the site of the blacksmith's shop established by Ron Brennand in 1903. If I try really hard, I can just remember him shoeing draught horses. Not that my recall is important, or even very reliable. What is important is the continuity, the live history, a reminder that rural life was once very different. Once, and not so long ago, it relied on the horse.

The Koppio museum also houses a special collection. In one of the side buildings is housed an astonishing display of barbed wire, donated by Port Lincoln resident and collector Bob Dobbins. It is a permanent collection and, as I now know, it contains more than barbed wire. A colleague at Macquarie University, geographer John Pickard, who has recently completed a PhD thesis on the history of fencing in Australia, writes therein of 'Bob Dobbins's superb collection of posts, droppers, wire, tools, etc . . .'.[16] The Dobbins collection, part of which is also on display at Tailem Bend, is surely unique, at least in South Australia, and probably Australia.

In an interview for this book Bob recalled how, after an article on his collection appeared in the *Port Lincoln Times* in 1985, local people dumped piles of fencing wire outside his house, which he then straightened and cut into display size of 18 inches (45 cm). He

The Koppio Smithy Museum.

mentioned the interest of telegraph employees too, and what made a good strainer post. Strainer posts and fencing wire may not appeal to everyone, but it is apparently a collectible and, as Bob said, 'every wire has a price', especially in America. Moreover, and this is the point here, the coming of fencing wire heralded a profound change in rural life. For one thing it meant the end of the shepherd, a vital figure in the pastoral age. Some shepherds may have been quite mad, due to isolation, but it was they who watched over the flocks and herds that made distant pastoralists rich and, as in the case of one Stubbs and his employer Biddle of Port Lincoln in the 1840s, bore the brunt of racial conflict arising from white settlement. Moreover, unlike most of the landholders, the shepherds actually lived on site. The coming of wire fencing in the late 19th century – some readers may recall the brand name Lysaght, which dates from the 1880s – was an augury of things to come. As with the blacksmith, the shepherd belongs to a bygone era.[17]

Not that change came evenly across the country. On the family farm in the late 1930s, shearing sheds might still have had stick fencing and thatched roofs. In many places, people and horses were still cheaper than machinery well into the 20th century. A lot of work would be needed to chart the decline of the rural workforce across the 20th century, though I have written about what happened on Brindabella Station, run by the Franklin family in New South Wales in the 1880s, and my farmer father used to say the biggest change in his lifetime – he was born in 1898 and died in 1975 – was the decline in the rural workforce. Regarding horses, the horse population of Australia peaked

'Kooltana' shearing pens and shed with thatched roof, featuring (left to right) Everard Carr and Pauline, John, Heather and Jean Roe, c. 1944.

at 2.5 million in 1919, but it would be many years before local museums became the chief repositories of the sorts of trucks and tractors found at the Koppio museum. In South Australia the last horse team was disbanded in the Mid North as late as 1958, and apparently there were still a few draught horses in agricultural areas in the 1960s.[18]

Closer settlement

The museum movement has been part of the enthusiasm all over the country for local and community history – the Pioneer Women's Hut at Tumbarumba in the Australian Alps is a good example – and it sometimes seems especially strong in South Australia, where the previous state celebration, Jubilee 150 in 1986, produced a great crop of local histories, including a number of nicely produced books on Eyre Peninsula, with catchy titles such as *Gum Trees and Gullies* (Yallunda Flat), *Grain amid Granite* (the Wudinna area), and *Between Lakes and Limestone* (a history of Kapinnie and Brimpton Lakes). Such works are invaluable in many ways and, like the local museums, evidence of a deepening self-awareness.

It is easy to forget how short the history of white settlement in the region really is. Although Eyre Peninsula has a European history which goes back to the sealers in the 1800s, it was a very lightly populated and mostly semi-arid region until the early 1900s. This was when farming in the north of the state failed as Goyder always said it would and, following closer settlement legislation in the 1890s, a minor folk movement from over Spencer Gulf to the south and west of the Peninsula occurred. Even today, however, the Peninsula is lightly populated and predominantly rural, with many of the smaller railway sidings now depopulated, and, with resident populations of

14,000, 22,000, and some 3000 respectively, Port Lincoln, Whyalla and Ceduna/Thevenard are the only sizeable urban spaces.[19]

It may be at this point that another historian would argue that technological change ensured the success of closer settlement in the early 20th century. Of course that was vital; so too was the prior state support in the case of 20th-century Eyre Peninsula and elsewhere, other examples in South Australia being the rail built across the eastern Mallee to Pinnaroo in the early 20th century, and the success of Coonalpyn Downs in the 1950s. On Eyre Peninsula the surveyors and fettlers and dam builders made life on the land manageable for the newcomers. They laid out the hundreds wherein small farming could begin, built the narrow-gauge railway from Port Lincoln to Minnipa and then Ceduna, and they constructed Tod River Reservoir in the Koppio Hills, from whence water was piped all the way up the Peninsula by 1928. But even so, that was not enough to secure rural communities.[20]

There were hard times to come, but at first they were only to be expected. I would suggest, however, that in addition to the technology, what ultimately ensured the success of closer settlement in this last of regions to be brought under the plough in the early 20th century was the skill of the people themselves. They were not novices. Their experience of the land did not extend as far back as in some other colonies, but it was profound. The big lessons came from the Far North, where planning was not enough. Nor was optimism about that mistaken mantra, 'rain follows the plough'. The people themselves had to work it out. As was long ago shown by D.W. Meinig, they had learned the hard way what was needed just to survive – as Meinig's classic title has it, *On the Margins of the Good Earth*.

They were also accustomed to hard physical labour, women and men alike. It killed too many of them too soon, especially the men. Both my grandfathers are buried in Port Lincoln cemetery, dead and gone by 1916, not much more than a decade on from their arrival. Of them I have almost no imagining, though it has become clear from reading Grandmother Roe's early diaries that her husband, Gilbert, who was far more interested in trading stock than farming, was lucky to have brought several competent workers from the lower north with him, and to have obtained a good block in the more fertile south. As for grandfather Heath, who died of double pneumonia in 1915 aged 44, it seems he was not much of a farmer either. Certainly he had no luck with access to good land, and there was no superphosphate in those days. Arriving with his family from the near north in 1905, he was unable to make things grow near Port Lincoln and when a few years later the family moved to land leased from the Mortlocks at Warratta Vale near Lipson, it was rain-shadow country and the soil was sandy. When he was allocated a block up north near Wudinna in 1915, it should have turned out well but, as noted earlier, both he and his son Roy died after a visit to the site that same year. In both cases, it was up to the widows to make a go of it – which they did.

Mention of grandparents reminds me of political journalist and historian Robert Murray's memoir, *Sandbelters: Memoirs of Middle Australia*. Murray's family finished up in suburban Sandringham in Melbourne, but they were up-country farmers in the Victorian Mallee first, and Murray has provided one of the richer and more realistic portrayals of that life to date; another such would be Penelope Hetherington's account of the Loveday family's attempt to establish itself at Chandada on the west coast during the interwar years in *The*

Making of a Labor Politician. (Some readers may recall Ron Loveday, the author's father, who later became Labor Minister for Education in South Australia.) In *Sandbelters*, Murray recalls the women of that first generation on the Mallee lands as matriarchs: 'They often approached life as the chief executive of a large household, eyes out for problems to overcome and for efficiency.'[21]

That struck a chord. My grandmothers were old and unwell by my time – they both died in the early 1950s, one aged 76, the other 84 – but they were held in awe by their large families, especially, it seemed, by the men, and Grandmother Roe's diaries are an eye opener for the modern reader. They are not grand, just a brief daily record of work and weather and incident, written up neatly with pen and ink in Woods' Daily Scribbling Diaries. It is from them that we know Gilbert Roe was usually off after the horses. One striking aspect of such records is the difference between men and women's work, and how much the latter did.

The discovery of a new source is the historian's delight. Whereas there are numerous published sources on the daily round of country men – one to be particularly recommended is Colin Thiele's *Sun on the Stubble* (1961), a portrayal of boyhood in the interwar years in the Barossa Valley – extended accounts by or about country women are less easily come by. More often their working lives are briefly touched upon in contributions to collections like *Eyre Peninsula Ramblings*, another Jubilee 150 publication, or survive in family records, such as Grandmother Roe's diaries.[22]

Here are some main points from Anna Roe's early diaries covering the years 1905 to 1907, when she was in her late thirties with six children and just settled on Lower Eyre Peninsula. Washing and ironing took up at least a whole day (though she seems to have had some kind of washing machine, a 'western washer' she called it, which she didn't think much of). Sewing and mending and darning for a large family could also fill up a whole day. Likewise, preparing for Sundays was a mammoth exercise. In the diary she records what they were all doing on Saturday 3 June 1905, some three months after their arrival – and by the way, the person referred to here and there as 'Dan' was Dan Singh, an Afghan worker they took over with them: 'Great shakes today – Dan grubbing Father carting some clay Jack drilling – and the cook very busy at the flour three turns of bread one of scones one of tarts one of pies one of biscuits and a big cake and 1 custard besides boiling meat vegetables & potatoes, and the Saturday work', with '(had 76 lbs [36 kg] beef)' added: an astonishing amount. Water remained a serious problem but somehow she quickly established a large garden too, including roses. It was quite normal for there to be up to 20 for Sunday lunch, or dinner as it was called then, mainly men. As she wrote in another entry, 'Providing for a growing family and four men besides so many chance callers called for a constant watch on supplies'. Apparently pickled beef was a standby. Mail went off once a week – a horseman would take the half dozen letters or more she had found time to send to the Indian Bolah Shah's general store over the hills for despatch. Letters were a lifeline. This touches on the issue of distance, a special paradox in centralising South Australia.[23]

From the 1920s

Rural society on Eyre Peninsula seemed to be shaping up well by the 1920s. In South Australia the Lower North and the Mallee communities were growing quantities of improved quality wheat, and new land in the granite belt around Wudinna in the north-west attracted young farmers from the south. Some research suggests that even returned soldiers did as well as could be expected. The land that Edward John Eyre had once described as 'a perfect desert' proved productive in places. At Kyancutta Robert Bedford set up his airline and advocated a new state; Mrs Birdseye's legendary bus service began; and the CWA (Country Women's Association) got going in Kimba. Best of all, there was by then a vast water reticulation system over almost the entire region, thanks to the EWS – the state's Engineering and Water Supply Service.[24]

The Great Depression put an end to all that exuberance. Farmers everywhere suffered the catastrophic fall in world wheat prices, and many left the land. What might have been the turning point in rural life – a new prosperity, the coming of machinery, richer social lives – was more like a false dawn. As for women on the land, their lives were improved in the sense that family sizes went down, but domestic work was barely affected so far beyond the cities, where electricity was starting to make a difference.

Women and men

Suddenly in the writing of this chapter I realise that, having been born in November 1940, I too might be regarded a child of the Depression years, that is if you define a decade as the ten years from 1931 to 1940. In that case, family life as I might have known it had not my mother died in January 1942 would have dated almost entirely from the Depression years. My parents were married at Wudinna in April 1933, and my three sisters were born in 1934, 1935, and 1937 respectively. But, of course, I was far too young and, as it happened, too remote, to have a sense of those prior years. As stated previously, when Edna Roe fell ill and was sent to Adelaide for treatment in late 1941, I was sent to her family up-country where I remained until 1945.

This is not a personal story or for that matter a family history, but aspects of both are relevant here. Although my grandmothers bore seven and eight children respectively, Grandmother Roe produced mainly boys – only one of two girls survived – while Grandmother Heath produced an equal number of boys and girls. Of those eight, however, two died young: her oldest child, Roy, who died in 1915 and the youngest of her four daughters, sixth-born Lily, who died of tuberculosis in October 1927, shortly before her 18th birthday, leaving Eric the oldest Heath child to survive, followed by Muriel, my mother, Edna, Auntie Isie and their brothers Doug and Tom. So it was that in the second generation, one side of the family was male-dominated and the other side seemed more female-oriented.

Edna was said to be the liveliest of the Heath sisters. She was born at Port Lincoln on 19 February 1905 and first worked for relatives at Tumby Bay as a shop assistant. Whether she ever lived up-country after her widowed mother and her siblings moved there in 1919 is unclear, but when the Wudinna Hospital opened in 1928 she became a nurse there, and later enrolled as a trainee nurse at the Royal Adelaide Hospital. That was prior to marriage in April 1933 and four children, born between 1934 and 1940. Soon after, she contracted pneumonia and then tuberculosis, from which she died in Adelaide on 13 January 1942, shortly before her 37th birthday. [25]

In late 1992, my sister Pauline forwarded a letter from the estate of my mother's older sister, Muriel, written by Edna Roe to her sister on 3 November 1941 from what was probably a chest clinic in Adelaide. It was the first time I had ever seen her handwriting or experienced her directly. It was a poignant letter, which she said should be put in the oven prior to reading to kill any germs, and at that stage it seems there was still the prospect of recovery. 'Why should it happen to me Muriel', she wrote, 'when I have my 4 dear little ones to look after besides being so happy in my married life . . . only God knows what a hard battle I have before me – looks like a six month job, perhaps longer.'[26]

I have mentioned before the ethos of those times that you must never feel sorry for yourself, but it does seem it was carried to extremes with us. Perhaps it was because, like her sister Lily, Edna Roe died of tuberculosis, still a stigmatising affliction and regarded as 'a dirty disease'. Perhaps it was because men like my father were so emotionally constrained at that time. Maybe I have repressed things. In any event, so far as I recall I never asked him about her, and as she died and was buried in Adelaide, it was not until I went there to school in 1955 that I visited her grave in the historic Cheltenham cemetery.

Auntie Isie took me there. By then Grandma Heath had died and Auntie Isie had moved to the city, where she began working as a cook-housekeeper. It is good to think that she earned enough in those later years to purchase a home unit in the suburb of Fullarton when she retired.

In retrospect, it seems that of those four Heath girls, only the oldest, Muriel, managed to live what would then have been regarded as a full life, having married, borne four children, and lived to a ripe old age in Perth. Moreover, although Grandmother Heath lived into her mid-70s, she had been widowed over 30 years earlier and was far from well in later years. At least her three remaining sons lived on, including the youngest, Tom, born in 1916, who served in World War II and lived to celebrate his 90th birthday.

Likewise, my grandmother Anna Roe lived on into the early 1950s, having been widowed at much the same time as Elizabeth Heath, and all her sons bar one lived to a good age, while her daughter Elizabeth, who was born in 1896 and died in 1961, lived longer than all but one of the Heath women. Maybe that was due to the more benign environment and better land on southern Eyre Peninsula.

The demographic approach just taken may have produced too bleak a view for the rising generation. In 1975, a rare personal account of rural life on Eyre Peninsula between the wars appeared in *South Australiana*, contributed by Joan Airy, who grew up just north of Cowell in the interwar years. It has a nice balance of self-respect and truculence – a tone I sometimes think is characteristically rural: 'We are on a farm because we like it and hope that the rural recession will never bea[t] us'. It did not beat her parents. Her father came from Kangaroo Island in 1911 and never owned the land that was, in any event, quite marginal. Nor did he ever make any money. But the way he and his wife managed their mixed farm through hard times is impressive. Nothing was wasted, and whatever food would grow, they grew. Joan Airy's mother could make soap and vinegar as well as meals and clothing; her father cut the family's hair, mended their boots, and nursed sick animals along with his farm work. The detailed account of Joan Airy's school days at Salt Creek School is especially valuable. Overall the Airy recollection may be taken to stand for a whole way of life in the country, now superseded.

There's no need to mourn its passing. Its significance here is that rural life took a battering as did the urban working class in the 1930s, but in some respects the country people were better off; they could survive more easily. And the good times were coming. I seldom go along with the idea that wars are for the good, but it must be admitted that war brought work at Whyalla for those less successful on the land, and primary production got a boost too.[27]

Then came the wool boom. Suddenly wheat-wool farmers became quite rich. We had the Korean War to thank for that: wars in cold climates were good for the wool industry. As well, a second, smaller round of soldier settlement proved much more successful than it had been after World War I. Moreover, contrary to expectations, the post-war boom lasted. Historians are agreed that a 'golden age of agriculture' eventuated in the 1950s and 1960s: for most families, country life was by then quite comfortable.

A turning point

Would the 1960s constitute a turning point for country life in the Eyre Peninsula? Maybe. But a balance between continuity and change is never easily struck. Even before then, the traditional markets for primary products such as wool were trending downwards; some areas of production have since closed down or been greatly cut back; and by now it is clear that the time has come to count the environmental costs. As well, a rising awareness of the claims of Indigenous people and knowledge of their ways is now challenging conventional wisdom on land use.[28]

Many people are now troubled by these developments, and rightly so, given the threat of economic decline and impending environmental change. However, the family farm has survived, albeit in changing guise and smaller numbers; many farmers are cognisant of the need for change; country women are more involved in farm management; there are new contributors to country life; and awareness of the importance of country is probably rising. Moreover, communications between town and country are set to improve and, whatever happens, country people are inclined to believe that the good times will come again.[29]

The South Australian historian Rob Linn ends his history of rural Australia over the past 200 years, *Battling the Land* (1999), on that very note, which is also a note of warning:

> Most [country] people believe that rural communities will recover from the slough of the recent past. Whichever way the winds of fortune blow for them, their history has been a prolonged battle between people and the land. A realisation of that struggle, and of the fact that environmental forces are the primary influence on life, lies at the heart of any true understanding of the story of rural Australia.[30]

Rural life may be more comfortable and some communities firmly established by now, but it is always tough at the margins, and fewer people now work the land. As Judith Brett argued in the essay cited at the beginning of this chapter, by the 1980s under market-oriented public policies people began to think the country probably did not matter much except for holidays, and maybe some foods. There certainly is a new interest in gourmet food and high quality ingredients, especially in South Australia and Tasmania.[31]

Perhaps things look different in South Australia, where the idea of a 'farmers' state' and the 'pioneer legend' outlined by John Hirst as long ago as 1978 live on. But I doubt it. Environmental degradation is a real issue everywhere, and distance is no protection these days from mindless market forces, even for Eyre Peninsula, and whatever happens, the production of food will be an ongoing issue. Now is the time to think about these things, and recognise that the resilience and adaptability country people have shown in the past will be vital to any effective response to the challenges that now confront us.[32]

In the meantime, for the residents of one of the driest regions of the driest state, water remains an issue. The story of water comes next.

CHAPTER 3

Water as a vital resource

creek – river – Goyder's line – pipeline – tanks and corrugated iron – some wider implications

Water has always been a vital issue on Eyre Peninsula. Place names are often derived from Aboriginal words meaning water, and the pattern of European settlement is closely related to its availability. In what follows, I take a look at some of the dimensions of water in the story of the Peninsula, starting from my own recollections of Kooltatta Creek and working back and forth over a remembered sequence of 'creek, river, pipeline', to end on a wider note of concern.

Creek

Kooltatta Creek is too small to appear on ordinary maps but its location may be inferred from the aerial photograph on a satellite map that appears on the web. This image indicates that the creek runs just north of Yallunda Flat in the Koppio Hills, and that it is located at the northern end of the Peninsula's highest rainfall belt, which we know from other sources has an average annual rainfall of between 400–500 mm (18–22 inches) p.a.

Here we are, my sister Heather and I, photographed at the bottom of the lane leading into the once family farm at Yallunda Flat in the spring of October 1997. We are standing by the sign announcing the

'Kooltana' signpost, me and Heather, October 1997.

property's name – it became the fashion to erect these signs in the 1950s – Kooltana being what we then thought was the name of the creek that runs through the property. It runs along the valley to our right, and the hills from which the creek arises can also be seen, in part. The creek, as we later learned, was originally called Kooltatta Creek, and is now once again known by this name.

Kooltatta Creek is an all-year-round creek, fed by small springs and run-off from rainfall. It is seldom, if ever, fast-flowing, and further down there are deep, clay-sided waterholes and dense, marshy flats to impede or block the flow but, unlike many creeks in this country, it does usually contain water. Altogether it is probably not more than three kilometres in length, and its depth varies with the soils through which it flows.

In Australia, as earlier in North America, the word 'creek' evolved far from its English origin as an inlet from the sea to encompass diverse types of watercourse, most of which are purely seasonal, as the explorer Charles Sturt put it in 1849 and is cited in the *Australian National Dictionary*:

> It may be necessary to remind my readers that a creek in the Australia colonies is not always an arm of the sea. The same term is used to designate a watercourse, whether large or small, in which the winter torrents may or may not have left a chain of ponds. Such a water course can hardly be called a river, since it only flows during heavy rains, after which it entirely depends on the character of the soil through which it runs, whether any water remains in it or not.

We were lucky to have a farm with such a creek, and to be at its headwaters, and I was lucky to have it as a playground. Some children living near local creeks could even pick native watercress, though it didn't grow in ours. I do dimly recall that potatoes once grew in a black soil patch. For Miss Tidy Mind, i.e. me, the chief pleasures were clearing out the smaller channels made by the springs on the sloping banks, and making sure the tiny waterfalls further down were working. These self-imposed tasks could take hours, during which time no one fussed about my whereabouts. In other places branches of the fringing sugar gums grew over the deeper pools and made nice diving platforms, and it was always possible to play 'black stockings' in the mud.

Young as I was during the years spent on the farm at Kooltana, I had reason to appreciate its attractions. Having spent the first five years of life at my maternal grandmother's farm, where the vegetation was mainly low mallee scrub and there was not a creek in sight, the contrast between the two places would be forever imprinted on my mind.

As the Council map of Koppio shows, Kooltatta Creek was just one of the many small watercourses to be encountered down south. Even so, it had four smaller tributaries of its own, and it in turn ran into a much longer creek from maybe as far north as the railway town of Ungarra. It was along the longer creek that now and then we went yabbying. The yabbies were quite big and unaccustomed to disturbance, so all you needed for a good catch was some old meat on a string, to dangle from the banks to the waterline where their holes were clearly visible, and a small net. We might have liked to do this more often, but it was quite a walk down the lane and involved trespass and maybe unknown stock.

Further downstream that longer creek would itself join another watercourse, the Yallunda Creek, which would in turn be joined by several tiny tributaries and, as it pursued its southward course, become the Tod Creek. Later again, once joined from the east by yet another somewhat longer creek, Pillaworta Creek, it becomes part of a river, the Tod River, Eyre Peninsula's only river and a short one at that, about which there will be more to say shortly. I knew its course quite well, as the road to Port Lincoln followed it for most of the way.

What with a reliable winter rainfall and the creeks, the people and productivity of the area were privileged by regional standards. Elsewhere on Eyre Peninsula sufficient water was often hard to come by, as explorers such as the doomed Charles Darke early found. During the first phase of European settlement, paucity of water limited activity to pastoralism. It would be an exaggeration to say that most of southern Eyre Peninsula was taken up by the Mortlocks, though their holdings at Coffin Bay and Tumby Bay were substantial, but it is worth mentioning that the whole of what is now the district of Ceduna was once one run, also that even the comparatively well-watered Cleve

Hills to the north near Cowell and just inside the Goyder line was a problematic area to farm at first. The early station memoir of the Cowell area, *Saga of Wangaraleednie*, is a vital document here.

Not surprisingly, the spread of settlement in the pastoral age was confined to the southern and western coasts of the Peninsula. Except for the Cleve uplands, there simply was not enough water for other forms of settlement or production. In addition to the creeks, there were other sources of above-ground water, but it was almost a century before the underground water resources of Uley-Wanilla outside Port Lincoln and the Polda Basin west of the centrally located railway town of Lock were brought into operation. In the meantime, at least until the imperatives of closer settlement in the early 20th century, finding the less obvious sources of water such as springs and soaks was a matter of Aboriginal know-how or white man's luck.

An infrequently remarked upon feature of Eyre Peninsula history is the wonderful place names, some of which have come up already, such as Pinkawillinie, south of Kimba. Many of the older names are Aboriginal in origin – how disconcerting to discover that the 'yalla' in Yallunda Flat is said to have meant 'violent' or 'hasty' – and many of them relate to water, as in Koppio and Ungarra.

Often overlooked is how much the earliest colonisers learnt about water from Aboriginal people. One who obviously did was pastoralist Thomas Magarey, who early on staked out a large holding south of Port Lincoln towards Sleaford Bay, known as Tulka. In an article for the South Australian Branch of the Royal Geographical Society dated 1895, entitled 'Australian Aborigines' Water Quest', Magarey wrote that many bushmen had benefited from Aboriginal watercraft. To read the article's outline of the ways in which they had collected and conserved water from time immemorial – from mallee roots and the hollows of she-oaks for example, and the morning dews on grasses and under sheltered rock, and in sand beds, rock holes and naturally occurring wells and caves – is to be mightily impressed. Moreover, and more simply, wrote Magarey, 'the presence of natives is always an indication to . . . whites of the proximity of water'. A similar story is told in *Saga of Wangaraleednie*. Having noted the springs and soaks around the settlement of that part of eastern Eyre Peninsula, the author goes on to say that the Aborigines 'knew how to obtain water from the roots of mallee and other shrubs and to take the dew as it fell' (p. 11). We know too that whalers, who for some 30 years prior to European colonisation camped for long periods along the harsh southern and western coasts, were able to rely on coastal rock seepages and underground supplies, though too little is known of them to say what they may have learned from the first peoples.[1]

Perhaps the best-known fact about the importance of water to the modern history of Eyre Peninsula is that there was not enough fresh water around Port Lincoln for it to be proclaimed the capital of the new province of South Australia, despite its grand harbour. As one who enjoyed 'Lincoln Springs' soft drinks as a child, I can testify that there was some fresh water to be had, but you have only to look at the bare hills in the background of the city to appreciate that there was not enough.[2]

The earliest European explorers and stockmen who followed the coastline east and west in the late 1830s invariably reported the absence of water. In 1839 that young gallant Edward John Eyre reported that on a journey around the whole triangle he had found none: 'during the whole of our course from Port Lincoln along the coast to Point Bell, and across the interior to the head of Spencer's [sic] Gulf, a distance of 600 miles through, I believe, an hitherto unexplored country, we never crossed a single creek, river or chain of ponds, nor did we meet with permanent water anywhere, with the exception of three solitary springs on the coast, to which the few natives we met appear to resort when the water left by the rain further inland has dried up.'[3]

Others also thought the coastal lands barren and useless, and felt their views were confirmed by the small number of natives they encountered. It would be a long time before an over-optimistic politician declared that the lands of the far west coast of South Australia would be another California, and longer still before the rich underground supplies of the Polda Basin came to the rescue.

River

Travels inland brought better news. In March 1839 an exploratory party led by Robert Tod set out in an optimistic mood and, four days' journey northwards from Port Lincoln, encountered a river, which they called the River Tod and followed westward over the hills, where they found plentiful fresh water and good grass. A few months later, one Captain Rawson was even more enthusiastic, reporting not only many thousands of fine acres with abundant water throughout the year along the Tod but more like it further north, where he claimed to have seen a veritable Mississippi of the south.[4]

It was not long before the promising lands were taken up on pastoral leases, some of which lasted until the 1940s. Large shearing sheds and outbuildings around homesteads with pleasant outlooks appeared along the creeks, as at Kapinka and Koppio, and jetties were built in sheltered bays along the nearby coasts to take the wool away.

Some pastoralists even built churches, as did the Mortlocks at Tumby Bay, where St Margaret's Church of England is still in use, and an almost feudal way of life emerged.[5] But the big men mostly lived in Adelaide, as historian John Hirst shows in *Adelaide and the Country* (1973), leaving it to overseers and solitary shepherds to mind the sheep. To me now, it is all rather reminiscent of Miles Franklin's homes at Tumut and Brindabella in Southern NSW, although her people were not absentees, and it was much colder there in winter.

Goyder's line

As is well known, in 1865 the Surveyor-General of South Australia George Woodroofe Goyder drew a 10-inch (300 mm) rainfall line across the State, beyond which agriculture could not be expected to flourish. Many reproductions showing the line do not include Eyre Peninsula. One that does is included here. It has the line running from below Cowell west to skirt the Gawler Ranges and beyond to peter out somewhere between Wirrulla and Ceduna. For a time I thought this was probably because Goyder never went there. Few had by then. But as a map from his office dated 1865 shows, some leases had been taken out in those parts by the 1860s – and I should have known better of this remarkable man, as important to regional and rural South Australia as Colonel Light is to Adelaide.[6]

Goyder's field notebooks are held in South Australia's State Records, and there in Volume 10 are the detailed notes on his journey to Eyre Peninsula in the winter of 1862. They show that he travelled up the west coast, from Port Lincoln to Fowlers Bay, visiting the big runs such as Talia, to the north-west of Elliston, as he went. This is the land of low rainfall and stone fences. At Fowlers Bay he noted the

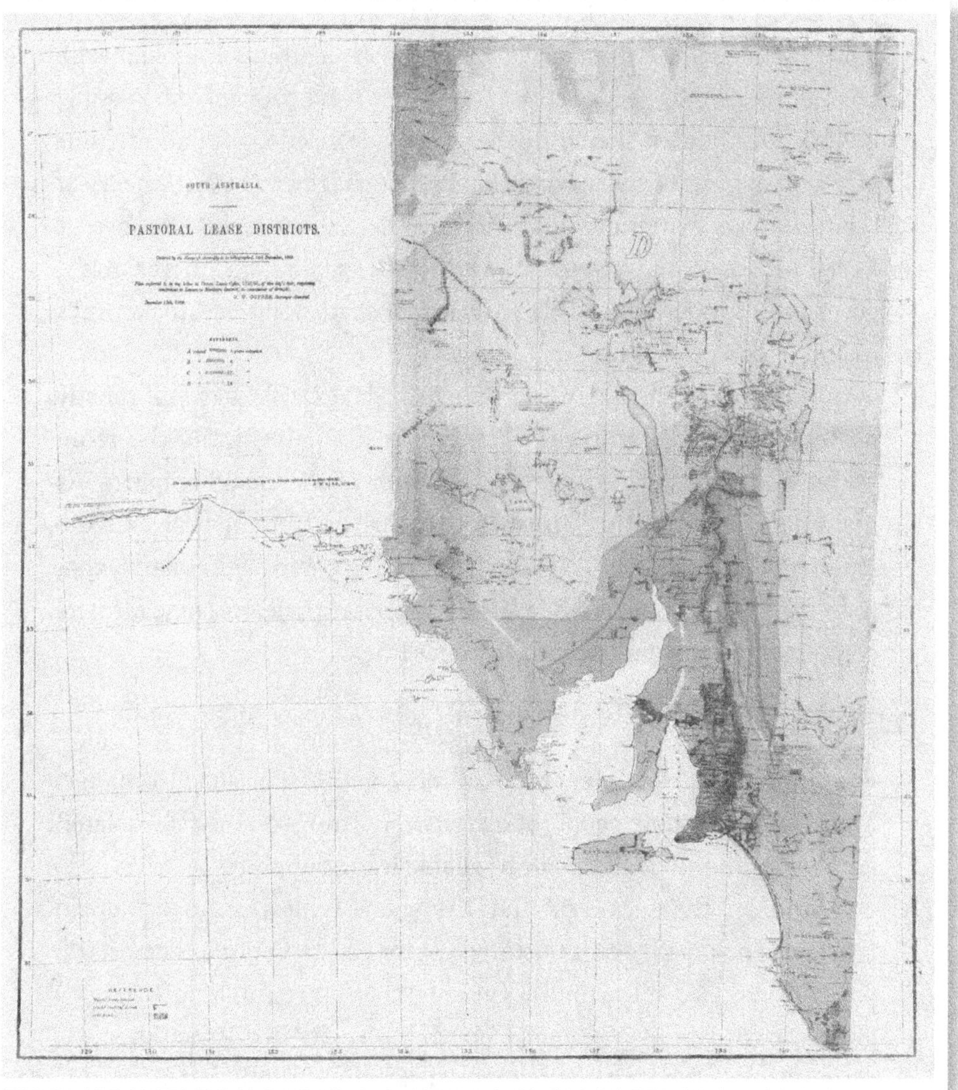

Goyder's map of South Australia's pastoral lease districts.
[SAPP 1865–66, no. 82, SLSA]

availability of water (and, importantly, if salty and whether or not his horses could drink it), and the grasses (mostly saltbush and bluebush). Further research is needed to ascertain if he went back inland. Possibly he did. An undated sketch in that overly detailed compilation-cum-angry panegyric, *Fading Footprints: Pioneers, runs and settlements of the lower Eyre Peninsula*, published by the author Jack Casanova at Port Lincoln in 1992, suggests that wells, soaks and, increasingly, government water tanks were early established along the stock routes to and from Port Augusta (p. 82).

With not much water and many salt lakes, this was still mostly pastoral lease land and, the further north one went and the more saltbush and bluebush there was, a matter of sheep and seaports. As many as 60 years would elapse before the wheat farming for which the Peninsula has until recently been best known could begin inland, and, thanks to drought and the depression, even longer before some farmers could make an income near to Goyder's line.

Pipeline

For farmers to make a go of it up-country, many things had to change. There had to be more people doing different things on the still-isolated Peninsula, and there had to be a reliable water supply.

So begins the story of the Tod Reservoir at Whites Flat in the Koppio Hills and the pipeline from nearby Knotts Hill to Ceduna/Thevenard, proudly described at the time as the longest water reticulation system by gravity in the world. Whether or not that is so, the Tod River scheme is certainly one of the great public works of the early 20th century in this country, and its construction and launch in just over a decade, between 1918 and 1928, is by today's standards quite impressive.

Arthur and Mary Wait and John and Jane Roe setting off with their families for a picnic at Tod Reservoir.

The reservoir proved to be a popular picnic spot. A family photograph survives of a group en route if I recall correctly in 1951 (it's hard to believe now that we sat on the wheat bags on the tray over those bumpy roads, but it was 1951, and all the roads were bumpy then). Once there, we would marvel at the retaining wall, an earthen embankment some 25 metres high and 351 metres long, with a vast water spread of over 130 hectares behind it, and, by looking down, we could see and appreciate the handsome 1920s style pumping station below. This regional reservoir would water the inland and make all the difference.[7]

In passing, it should be noted that Eyre Peninsula was not the only area of Australia where a large reservoir was constructed in

The Tod River Pumping Station. [*Walkabout*, April 1948]

the early 20th century. For example, the mighty Burrinjuck Dam in the Australian Alps south of Goulburn dates from 1907. The 1890s drought, especially in the eastern states, was one variable in the spate of dam building. The call for an increased population was another, as was unremitting urban growth and the ongoing demand for land after the gold rushes of the 1850s. But in rural history, the transition from a pastoral age to closer settlement was most important. In the case of Eyre Peninsula, it was the failure of farming lands beyond Goyder's line to the north of Port Augusta in the 1880s, when hubris set in among those who 20 years earlier had confidently asserted that 'rain follows the plough', which marked the transition.

A folk movement south and west, around or across Spencer Gulf to the lands where pastoral leases were running out and the prospects seemed good, began in the 1890s. Koppio Station offers a case in point, and of some bearing, in that the tiny village of Yallunda Flat dates from this transition, with the first settlers and an Indian-run shop established by 1907, and even a one-teacher school. It was through Yallunda Flat that my grandparents Gilbert and Anna Roe from upper Yorke Peninsula had made their way in carts from the landing at Tumby Bay over the hills to Marble View in 1905. According to Anna Roe's diary, it took several trips to get settled in what used to be called 'virgin bush'.

Such cumbersome links with the wider world were gradually remedied. The train line, which was up and running from Port Lincoln to Cummins by 1907 and the final section, from Nunjikompita to Thevenard, by 1915, was vital to the problem of water, but the solution took time. When amateur natural scientist 'Professor' Robert Bedford arrived at Kyancutta with his family by train in 1915, he soon found, as his diary puts it, that 'water was a serious problem'. He had just sunk a 15 foot well and got only salt water. His wife Hilda recorded the travails of other would-be settlers: 'During 1915–16 settlers came from quite long distances with their goods and chattels in the [covered] wagons . . . One settler and his wife arrived with all they possessed in a spring cart – six children and two bags of flour.' The reticulated water that had been promised in 1915 did not arrive until 1926, Bedford noted crossly. In the meantime it was up to the settlers to find or cart water for their stock and themselves.[8]

When it came, the iron and concrete pipeline ran above ground as far as Minnipa and alongside the railway line from west of Knotts Hill to Thevenard – approximately 380 km. Altogether, the two projects cost the state a considerable amount of money, but both the rail and the water were needed if the region was to progress, and the reservoir does not seem to have been a controversial proposition by the time the Royal Commission reported in August 1916 on *Eyre's Peninsula Water Supply*. The Commissioners found that a general water supply system was crucial:

> No other extensive portion of South Australia is so severely and supremely in need of a permanent water supply as Eyre's Peninsula. Unless provision is made in this direction without delay, disastrous settlement, especially in the hundreds which have been opened up in recent years, [is] inevitable. In the absence of an adequate water supply the development of vast areas of agricultural and grazing land will be seriously retarded.[9]

The Commissioners had seen for themselves the hardships experienced by recent arrivals on the dry lands after the construction of the railway, and wondered at the tenacity of some while emphasising that many would be obliged to abandon their holdings if nothing was done. As well as this, Port Lincoln needed more water for both domestic use and waste disposal, and a steady supply for the steam trains at the rail terminus. Up-country, the cost of water cartage was astronomical. Some places, they wrote, were 'worthless without water'.

It is striking how firm the tone of the report is. Clearly the Tod River Scheme had to proceed. Reticulation along the east coast was also envisaged. The underground supplies of the Polda Basin were noted, but it was feared that they would be too easily depleted, and that the water would become too salty. To that issue we must in due course return. The three small catchments near Cleve were known to be inadequate.

The Tod River Reservoir. [*Walkabout*, April 1948]

As told in an undated typescript on the development of water supplies on Eyre Peninsula in my possession, probably compiled by Water Supply bureaucrats, work began under contract on the reservoir in 1918. However, the contracted firm soon fell into financial difficulties and, in 1919, with local entrepreneur Joseph Timms, Sidney (later Sir Sidney) Kidman was appointed by the South Australian Commissioner of Public Works to take over. The reservoir was built by 1922, but the laying of pipes to Ceduna/Thevenard (by other contractors) took a further five years, from 1923 to 1928. Such was the significance of the project's completion, the then Commissioner of Public Works, the Hon. M. McIntosh MP, went all the way over to Ceduna for an official opening in June 1928.[10]

It was not long, however, before the supply from the Tod was inadequate, and new sources were needed. By the mid-1930s reconditioning work was needed too. By 1949 the Uley-Wanilla Basin was in full operation, with automated bores at work supplementing the Tod and the east coast line (which dates from 1930 and was built to support the smaller catchments near Cleve as well as to serve the farming communities along the way). Soon after, the main trunk line supply was boosted by water from the Polda Basin for the north and later the east. Reticulated water finally reached Kimba in 1973, the town having suffered restrictions and costly cartage for years before.[11]

Tanks and corrugated iron

The humble water tank appears in many photos of farms in the interior during the years of closer settlement, and later. As I recall, we had three around the house at Kooltana in the 1950s. It is probably still an essential item these days. So too were – and probably still are – water troughs. It's important to remind ourselves that clean fresh water is vital to the wellbeing of both people and stock, also that until mechanisation took command with the coming of tractors and the like, the hard work was done by horse teams. Again I can dimly recall maybe 12 draught horses that had be fed and watered daily. Likewise, transport and communications were horse dependent until at least the 1920s; to collect the mail on brumby 'Mick' or semi-draught 'Nigger' (yes, he was black) was one of the delights of my childhood.

In the mid-20th century the magazine *Walkabout* ran two articles that highlighted the positive effect of a reliable water supply on this part of the world. In the first, published in April 1948 and entitled 'Water for Mallee lands', author Michael Harland celebrated transformation: 'the water main . . . brought salvation to the mallee . . . made industries possible, saved stock, . . . assured household water supplies, and brought colour into gardens where flowers rarely grew before. No longer is the mallee dry!' (p. 36). The second article was by the West Australian novelist Katharine Susannah Prichard, who traversed the Peninsula by road en route from Perth in 1964 and found the country blooming, rather like the West Australian wheat belt – a considerable compliment at the time.

Such enthusiasm needs to be modified. I have already pointed to some of the main ways in which the pipeline itself had to be boosted over time. For some people, especially in the years before Harland's article, the good times never came. By 1948 the unlucky ones had moved away, to Port Lincoln, or Whyalla, maybe even Adelaide. In *The Making of a Labor Politician: Family and politics in South Australia 1900–1980* (1982), in my view one of the best books yet on the Eyre Peninsula experience, Penelope Hetherington shows how between 1928 and 1936 her parents Ron and Liza Loveday tried hard to make a go of it on a block at Chandada, west of Cungena, only to be defeated by drought and the collapse of wheat prices. The experience radicalised them, and by 1938 the family was settled in Whyalla, where Ron entered Labor politics.

How well do I recall the corrugated roofs and tanks still to be seen in what remained of the Loveday's three-roomed house at Chandada in 2013. There was probably a corrugated iron loo out the back too. It reminded me that water could be collected on iron roofs and stored in corrugated iron tanks for household use. Corrugated iron has been an iconic building material on Eyre Peninsula, as elsewhere in Australia. Certainly it was a godsend on the frontier, being cheap, light, durable, recyclable, and portable too, but as a building material it was also very hot in summer and cold in winter.

The remains of the Loveday house at Chandada, 2013.

Stories and images comparable to those of the Lovedays may be found in the community histories produced in 1986 for Jubilee 150, and scattered through rural memoirs, for instance Wilf Roediger's *We Survived* recounts a search for water in summer.[12] But it's time to turn to Whyalla. The story of Whyalla presents a dramatic example of the role of water in the development of Eyre Peninsula.

The opposite photo of Whyalla, which also appears in Peter Stanley's very enjoyable 2004 account of *Whyalla at War*, gives some idea of its early working-class character. (Peter Stanley, who is now a leading military historian, grew up at Whyalla.) It may not be easy to fully appreciate as a place, but it is by far the largest city on the Peninsula (22,000 at the 2011 census), and it has a distinct history as the only industrial city, despite being situated on the southern edge

View of Whyalla and Broken Hill Proprietary Works, 1933.
[SLSA B 8605]

of the same semi-arid lands of the north that Goyder warned about. Striking as the rich iron-bearing hills beyond are – or were – it is a harsh environment, with not a creek to be seen.

So how did 'the red city' survive? Rainfall seldom exceeds 260 mm (10") p.a., and the Peninsula's southern-based water system does not reach so far north. An answer was a long time coming. BHP was involved before 1900, and growth was steady from World War I onwards, but right up to the 1940s residents of Whyalla had to rely on supplies brought in by bullock drays from near Iron Knob or by barges from Port Pirie, plus water brought as ballast from Newcastle. It was the building of a blast furnace and shipbuilding during World War II that forced the issue. Construction of the Morgan–Whyalla pipeline began in 1941 and was completed in 1944.

Some wider implications

How symbolic it seems that Whyalla's water supply comes from Morgan on the River Murray, and the story of water on Eyre Peninsula is thereby linked with the larger issue of water from the Murray–Darling system. A great deal has been written about the Murray–Darling system as it reaches South Australia, though not so much as I am aware on its possible effect in such far-flung places as Whyalla and Streaky Bay. The national debate begins in Queensland and, with the extensive irrigation projects now functioning there, is unlikely to be resolved in the short term.

Meanwhile the system that began in the Koppio Hills way back in the 1920s faces its own challenges. As noted earlier, the Tod Reservoir was finally shut down in 2004 and has yet to be reopened. At first I found this news quite shocking. But then I remembered how, when visiting in January 2007, I saw that several small dams had been built on farmlands along the various creeks' tiny tributaries, and that there was a wizened appearance to the Kooltatta Creek itself. At the time I thought it was due to the season. Now I'm not so sure. There has always been a salinity problem along the west coast of South Australia, as there is in the farmlands of Western Australia, but surely there should not be one in the Koppio Hills? According to *Dryland Salinity Management in the Tod River Catchment*, a discussion paper-cum-handbook produced by a land-care group in June 2000 and now available on the web, the main contributing factor has been land clearing, notably along the creeks and gullies. And what if mining for iron ore gets underway along the east coast of the Peninsula, as may well happen? One map I have seen shows possible lodes extending south well into the Koppio Hills. What this might do to the ancient watercourses and the catchment areas is anyone's guess. Currently a new port is planned for Sheep Hill to the north-east of historic Lipson and two others are in the offing nearby.

I had intended to end this discussion of water as a vital resource for Eyre Peninsula on a more cheerful note. Maybe I still can, but it is probably more appropriate to say that water as a theme in the history of the Peninsula is entering a new phase. With luck, it might see a return to the collectivism that characterised the agricultural phase, and the coming of a closer attention to the environment. It does seem improbable though. According to the mining company Centrex, eastern Eyre Peninsula is an emerging iron and minerals province.[13]

Whatever the future may hold, water as an issue is unlikely to go away. It has a sobering history for the whole country, and as the local MP Peter Treloar said when seeking an inquiry into the water supply on Eyre Peninsula in 2011, no other issue has created the same degree of interest and passion in his electorate.[14]

Some developments are indeed startling. Not only has the Tod Reservoir been mothballed since 2004 but pumping of the Polda Basin ceased in 2006, and the Morgan–Whyalla pipeline has recently been extended from Whyalla/Iron Knob to Kimba and beyond. Apparently Streaky Bay now takes 20 per cent of its water from that source.

If I read local concerns correctly, the coming of the miners focused anxiety about a decline in the quality and quantity of ground water on Eyre Peninsula. Some attributed it to over-use, others to rainfall fluctuation and administrative problems. The debate led to the inquiry sought by Peter Treloar in 2011 and a substantial report by the state's Water Resources Committee two years later. Published in October

2013, the Committee wisely avoided recriminations and, in looking to the future, sought a balanced view of the problems of the past. The positive approach was appreciated, and the suggestion that the Tod Reservoir might be re-opened has been warmly welcomed.

Important as such possibilities are, many of the issues are ongoing, and it may be that Eyre Peninsula will be one of the first places to show what the limits of growth are likely to be.

CHAPTER 4

The school bus

the subject – our bus – the one-teacher school – the area school – the challenge – the school bus revisited

This is not about those big yellow buses you sometimes see ferrying city children to their preferred schools. It is about country kids and rural schools in remote South Australia in the 1940s and 1950s, where my own schooling began, and how we got to school, which could be no small challenge.

Our bus

My three older sisters first went to school in a jinker, as in the photograph on the next page. It was probably taken when they were setting off for Yallunda Flat Primary School, a tiny one-teacher school in the Koppio Hills, where I would soon join them. As I recall, we tied the horse under a tree with a nosebag of chaff for the day. Pauline, the oldest of the four of us, drove the two-and-a-half miles along a dirt road there and back each day from a young age. It may not sound like it but, except when it rained, it was a lovely trip, with sugar gums, wattle and she-oaks lining the road, and rarely any traffic.

The school bus came a little later, when both Pauline and Jean were ready for secondary schooling at Cummins, the railway town some 20 kilometres to the west over the hills. (Before that, to continue

Off to school in a jinker, (left to right) Pauline, Jean, and Heather Roe, and Mary Low, baby daughter of the teacher who boarded with us.

at secondary level Pauline had ridden her bike over the hills to pick up a Cummins school bus on Monday mornings, stored the bike in a nearby farmer's shed, boarded in town for the week, and on Friday afternoons caught the bus back again, collected her bike, and rode home for the weekend.) Happily a photograph of the first Yallunda Flat bus dated c. 1948 survives – though as can be seen, it was not much like a bus, even by the standards of the day. The owner-driver Mr Durdin, a retired carrier resident at Yallunda Flat suitably remunerated by a state subsidy, has put a tarpaulin or canvas cover over the tray of a Ford V-8 truck, presumably adding a stepladder at the rear for access. As recalled by Pat Green (previously Laube), there was seating around the edge of the tray and space for school bags in the middle. Possibly the truck was

The first Yallunda Flat-Cummins schools bus and passengers, (left to right), back row: Gavin Mason, Elaine Laube, Pauline Roe, Jean Ford, Jean Roe, Ian Lear, John Lear; middle row: Bob Hughes, Heather Lear, Pat Laube, Trevor Laube; front row: Peter Blacker, Sam Armunim, Meryl Lear. [Pat Green]

army surplus, and I would not be surprised to learn that the seating consisted of wheat bags filled with sawdust.[1]

Yallunda Flat school bus number two, which most of us remember, was also driven by Mr Durdin. It was somewhat more suited to the task – a Dodge or Fargo utility with its back covered in by a wooden framed box and wooden planks bolted to the floor around the sides, except at the rear, where double doors opened to let down steps for the children to climb aboard. It was up to the older ones to manage the steps and maintain order along the way.

The trip to Cummins took about an hour each way, with delays for picking up children en route and sometimes having to wait for them to reach the pick-up point from side roads or, as in our case, come rushing out of the house with school cases and hair ribbons flying. At its peak, some 20 children fitted onto our bus, with a couple of the later pick-ups seated in the front by the driver. There was a window from the cab to enable the driver to see what was going on, though Pat Green says the children did their best to block it off.

The school at Cummins began as an elementary or primary school in 1912 and became an all-age area school in 1942. Yallunda Flat Primary School, which it seems began as Koppio School and was renamed in 1907, lasted a little longer than most, but by May 1951 there were only five pupils left (of whom I was one) and it was closed. According to the rules, six were needed to keep it open. How it lasted so long I cannot say, but parental support for these public schools had been encouraged in the 1940s, and every effort was made in most parts of rural Australia to keep the one-teacher schools open, since the journey over rough unmade roads was thought to be hazardous and tiring for young children. At one stage my oldest sister, Pauline, was sent a good way north on her bike to help keep a school on Chinmina Hill open, and in 1945 Jean went down to Koppio School to add to enrolments there (in fact, Pauline's rides were unavailing and the Chinmina school was closed, but the Koppio school lasted until 1970). Furthermore, the school buildings were often a focus of community life. That was certainly true of our little school.

By 1951, all of my three sisters had undertaken or were undertaking secondary education at Cummins, and I was a healthy 10-year-old, soon to be deemed ready for the trip. During my later years at Yallunda

Flat Primary School, there was no need for the jinker. We younger children could catch a ride there on the school bus that carried our elders to Cummins. It meant getting to school early, by about eight in the morning, but there was plenty to do, especially on Monday mornings, when there were refundable drink bottles to collect from the nearby showground and cash in at the general store down the road – the store whose origins date back to Indian trader Bolah Shah in the early 20th century. It also meant a long wait in the afternoon, so that often it was quicker to walk home, partly along the road, and partly across the paddocks past the original school site on the hillside by the Stokes road, a location which incidentally made it easy for me to recognise the site of Miles Franklin's 1890s school on the hillside at Thornford, south-east of Goulburn, when I went looking for it in 2002.

The Yallunda Flat Store and Post Office in 1905.

[*Gum Trees and Gullies*]

Such agreeable arrangements could not last. On 15 May 1951, after what now seems an astonishing turnover of mainly very young female teachers – not surprisingly they seldom stayed more than nine months – and with few new enrolments in sight, the Yallunda Flat Primary School was finally closed, having had some 22 teachers overall, 7 of them male, 15 female. From then on it was the school bus all the way to Cummins and a new educational experience. I was by then in grade six and, unlike sister Heather, I never rose to be captain of the school bus because, having completed what was then called grade nine, due to changes in family life to be mentioned later, in 1955 I was sent to finish my schooling in the great city – the one city – of Adelaide. But I had almost four years on the bus, which was quite long enough to get the hang of things.

The historian is lucky to find a passing reference to the school bus in general histories, but does better in state educational histories and local newspapers, and it sometimes surfaces in memoirs or as an aspect of an oral history. Literary evidence is often the best. One striking instance occurs in the late Randolph Stow's semi-autobiographical *The Merry-go-round in the Sea* (1965, p. 117), a classic work that deals with boyhood in Geraldton, Western Australia, in the 1940s. For Stow, with the bus it's a song and the road that matter. So it was for me, and more, and although I cannot hope to write like Stow, I do take heart from his account, which I happened upon by chance not long ago.

In Stow's story, the boy is on the bus singing a 1940s hit, which I remember quite well:

> You are my sunshine, my only sunshine,
> You make me happy when skies are grey . . .

and so on, to

You'll never know, dear, how much I love you:
Please don't take my sunshine away.

'The school bus rang out,' he writes, 'with the singing. The school bus was beautiful, like a chariot', and as it progresses along the flat-topped range they sing another to me familiar song:

The oy-ul wells
Are full of smells
Deep in the heart of Texas.

And on they went, deep into the heart of Texas until the boy felt, when they crossed the range, they were going 'towards the heart of mythical Australia'.

The Ford ute from Yallunda Flat was no chariot, but it was as true for us as for Stow that the bus was a microcosm of our world and 'The landmarks were children . . . getting on and off the bus'. And it was fun. On the bus I tried learning to yodel. We all listened to the hillbilly half hour on the radio, station 5DN as I recall, and Mavis Walter, who liked to dress as a cowgirl, actually could yodel. Every morning between 6.30 am and 7 am the station played Tex Morton and others doing their stuff. Could one song have been 'China Doll': 'I'm tired of crying/and all your lying/my China doll'?

Even catching the bus was fun. I've previously mentioned the Roe sisters' rush to get on in the mornings, bags and hair flying. And here is Pat Green's account of shenanigans along the way (which shows incidentally that I haven't changed that much): 'you . . . spent most journeys swotting up on geography . . . the rest of us were more interested in boys or getting into fights'.

Along the way to Cummins, the bus would halt at sheltered spots by the side of the road to pick up the waiting children, in ones and twos and sometimes even threes and fours. Not many came from Yallunda Flat, but once over Cabot's Hill, where would-be cowgirl Mavis got on, into the more mallee-like lands, the numbers increased. I used to think that sometimes, as we drew close to our goal, the bus would pick up some Aboriginal children, 'the Betts kids' we called them, but I've since been told that their camp was south of the town, not east, where we came in from.

Aboard the bus, the order of seating was a serious matter, with the littlest nearest the front of the bus and the rest ranged along the sides according more or less to age and when people got on. The best seats were of course the two by the back doors, taken by the boy who managed the door and the bus captain, who was supposed to keep order and was responsible in the afternoons for checking that everyone was there to join the homeward-bound bus.

After school at Cummins, everyone would line up on the asphalt in the schoolyard to be counted. Since ours was the smallest bus, we often managed to win the daily competition to get away first. But it could be a hollow victory. If the driver was a bit late, we might find ourselves having to wait along the footpath, though it was never for long. By five o'clock we were all back home, busy with the jobs country kids had to do in those days: milking cows, collecting eggs, finding firewood, chopping wood and setting tables.

With some 20 kilometres to traverse, the Yallunda Flat bus probably had the shortest route of the area school buses. Altogether the school was served by six feeder buses: in addition to our bus from the east, the Wildeloo and Cockaleechie buses came in from the north/

Lined up waiting for the bus after school

north-east, the Yeltukka bus from the Kapinnie/Brimpton Lake area to the west, the Pilanna bus from the imposing ranges to the south-west, and Edillilie from the south. The wonderful place names were mostly of Aboriginal origin and, as discussed previously, often a variant on 'water' – a spring, a soak, a swamp, maybe a waterhole – a notable exception being Cockaleechie, from the name of a Scottish soup.

In small situations everyone matters, and each has a readily discernible personality. As the children got on the bus they would be greeted with interest – perhaps something unusual had happened on the farm in the past 24 hours? And often it had. Not much could be expected of the bus driver's granddaughter, who got on first. Her mother, said to have been an opera singer, was now divorced and temporarily returned to the family fold; we thought her daughter was probably a bit above herself. It was the same for the next girl, an only child whose hard-working parents had the misfortune to be mere dairy farmers and who was different: she was good at art, not sport. These two went on to respectable careers, one as a Uniting Church minister and the other as a professional photographer. Another of those early bus kids, Peter Blacker, became the long-serving state member for Flinders, representing the National/Country Party, and there's me, the only one so far as I know to make it to university. I may have mixed feelings about some of those early experiences, but I have no time for patronising and anachronistic attitudes to country people.

The one-teacher school

My first school at Yallunda Flat was a one-teacher school. The heyday of the one-teacher school in Australia came in the 1930s. According to Hank Nelson, some 140,000 out of a million Australian schoolchildren, that is almost 15 per cent, were being educated in one-teacher schools in 1930, and there were some 7000 such schools nationwide. Of these, a high proportion (about 700) were in South Australia, where some 80 per cent of all primary schoolchildren were attending state schools, a proportion which increased in the 1940s and again in the 1950s, reaching 83 per cent in 1945 according to Colin Thiele. Thiele also estimated that there were more one-teacher schools in South Australia in the 1920s than the 1930s (800), over half of them enrolling fewer that 20 pupils. This was no doubt due to the extent of closer settlement; further out, in less densely settled areas there and elsewhere, families relied on travelling teachers and correspondence courses (and later the School of the Air). Sometimes these were only interim services: in the 1920s at Laura Bay, south of Ceduna, farmer's wife Mary Blumson taught her three children with the aid of correspondence lessons until 1927 when a school was established locally.[2]

If it was true in dry old South Australia that the frontier dream, whereby rain follows the plough, was well and truly dead by the early 20th century, it was nonetheless the case that the one-teacher schools kept on. But it was not for long. A careful documentation of one-teacher schools in one area of Eyre Peninsula undertaken by the Kimba Historical Society in 1986 shows that there were over 20 one-teacher schools within 40 kilometres of Kimba in the 1920s, when farming began around there, but that by the 1940s most of them had closed. (My favourite would have to be Pinkawillinie South, though I couldn't find the site when I went looking for it in 2007.) The young Harry Schiller was a pupil at two such schools to the north-east of Cowell in the early 20th century; no keen pupil, he was handicapped at the outset because he could only speak a mixture of German and English, but he would sympathise with the hardships experienced by 'lady teachers' and was appreciative of the role played by the school buildings in the life of the tiny communities there, as elsewhere, for meetings, dances and church services ('everyone attended').[3] In the Franklin Harbour region to the south-east of Kimba, which has recently been studied by Kay Whitehead and fellow researcher Ben Wadham, there were as many as nine one-teacher schools in 1900, the sites of which are now marked by concrete mileposts, thanks to an initiative of the Franklin Harbour National Trust in the 1980s.[4]

Although it was located in a cooler, wetter, more fertile and older area of European settlement, Yallunda Flat Primary was more or less typical of the one-teacher schools on the Peninsula. It may have lasted longer than most of the schools in the Kimba area, but it too had to close eventually. When it opened as Koppio school in 1905 there were as many as 26 pupils, but by 1932 there were only 11 enrolments, and in 1942 numbers were down to seven. By 1951, when as previously mentioned it was closed, it had fallen to five. Likewise, it had a run of mainly young women teachers straight out of college who were paid a pittance and had to board with local families. Most of them stayed for short periods, though I can recall one older male teacher who lasted three years: he was my first teacher and we admired him because he was a nice man with a tiny red car and he smoked cigarettes. After him came three girl teachers and one or two males of variable quality. By then at least the school had a decent fence and two dunnies, as they were called, down the back yard, most of which was covered by a smelly evergreen shrub of American origin known as stinkweed, which left little enough space for PE (Physical Education) and for playing farms round the edges, as we liked to do at recess. Nor was the school garden up to much by then, being overshadowed by a giant pine tree, a tree favoured for shade and as a windbreak at that time (though in drier parts it was more likely to be the droopy pepper tree).

Like many one-teacher schools, Yallunda Flat Primary had a chequered history of openings and closures, but the temporary weatherboard structure built there in 1930 lasted to the end. The building was standard issue from Adelaide – this was a highly centralised system. I have two graphics of pupils lined up outside the school in the mid-1940s. The photograph that was taken in 1944 has my three older sisters, who make up half of the necessary six enrolments (the boy in the tie was a ring-in from Melbourne and the baby belonged

The 1944 enrolment at Yallunda Flat School.

[*Gum Trees and Gullies*]

The 1948 enrolment at Yallunda Flat School.

[*Gum Trees and Gullies*]

to the teacher, a young woman whose husband was in the army). In the next graphic it seems enrolments have picked up briefly with 12 children pictured, and the two on the right are bare-footed (and they walked to school). To my surprise, Heather and I are neatly dressed in school uniforms. Presumably they were hand-me-downs, as both our older sisters were now over the hill at Cummins Area School, where uniforms were the norm (and a relief from the anxiety about what to wear to school each day).

What we learned at our one-teacher school is now no longer even a memory, but it was probably quite a lot. If I recall correctly there was only one shelf of so-called library books, and only two titles I can remember reading, one on Hereward the Wake by Charles Kingsley, the other *Captains Courageous* by Rudyard Kipling, and I don't recall any music, though there was surely some. The coming of school broadcasts made a difference with programs such as 'The World We Live In', as did the monthly distribution of a free departmental publication from Adelaide called *The Children's Hour*, founded way back in 1889 to enhance the reading experience of schoolchildren – which in many cases was badly needed (though not by me as my father was a reader, regularly borrowing books from a library in Port Lincoln). Even by this time, teachers in more remote schools sometimes found themselves having to teach standard speech to the children of farmers, some of whom could neither read nor write, and personal hygiene was everywhere emphasised, including handkerchief drill. Given the outdoor cesspits and buckets that all too often served as toilets up the country, hand washing under taps from the water tank was of some importance. Mostly though we admired the teachers, who returned from holidays in the city with new clothes and novelties, such as a fountain pen. Status in those schools was enhanced by the possession of such items. How wonderful it was to be given a box of Lakeland colour pencils one birthday, and a ruler with samples of Australian timbers such as silky oak on another.

Actually my most vivid memories of those school days are not of the lessons, but of playing farms in recess – 'little' it was called. 'Little' was not so much a game as an activity based on the seasons and what was happening on the farms around us, and I will have more to say about it shortly.

It has been suggested by students of autobiography in Australia that we are best at the early years. There are plenty of examples. I was interested to compare my own recollections with for example those of Adelaide journalist Max Fatchen, who recalled walking to school as 'a time for contemplation', and those of Alan Frost in his *East Coast Country: A North Queensland Dreaming* (1996), where he also remembers games and the spirit of place better than his lessons. Another example would be Patsy Adam-Smith's classic memoir *Hear the Train Blow* (1964), which is especially telling on pupil–teacher interaction. Nonetheless, it is a rare thing to come upon an appreciative outline of the school day, as vividly recalled by Joan Airy, who, as previously noted, attended a one-teacher school to the north-east of Cowell in the interwar years. More familiar is the testimony of that rather austere Western Australian historian Penelope Hetherington, who feels she learned little at her bush school up the line at Cungena, and writer Janette Turner Hospital, who, having attended a Brisbane primary school in the mid-1950s, found intellectual stimulation came later. Girls especially were caught in a gender trap though we didn't know it at the time.[5]

An interesting aspect of these recollections is that, by and large, the students recall their teachers with affection. Max Fatchen is not the only one to mention how good the class was when the inspector arrived, as far as they knew unexpectedly, though the teacher should have been informed. The inspection system was pretty thorough then, and terrified teachers well into the 1950s. According to one man's jaundiced testimony, the inspectors forgot that they had once been teachers, though he may have been a bit of a curmudgeon himself. Years later at Adelaide Girls High School, I recall how Mrs Kearney, the top Latin teacher, one day suddenly paused to send a girl up the street to buy flowers for the classroom as the inspector was coming. Spare a thought for those isolated young teachers in the bush who had to face many hazards, such as boarding with families, some welcoming, others not; getting to the school under their own steam, by bike or buggy or even shanks's pony; and professional isolation. They could expect to spend their first five or six years at places they had never heard of, and possibly under dire circumstances, as in one recorded instance having to sleep in the shed that served as the family's main living area, with only a curtain for privacy.[6]

But there's no need to be too sentimental. Most teachers enriched their communities immeasurably, and sooner or later many of the women teachers married local farmers.[7] Even though married women were then excluded from teaching in state schools, some exceptions were made.

The problem for a historian with most one-teacher schools is that their records generally do not survive. Efforts to locate those for my own one-teacher school have been unavailing. But some do, and, happily, some of those of the school at nearby Koppio are available

The Koppio School. [Koppio Museum]

(though access after 1951 is restricted). Koppio is by now just a name on a map denoting several road junctions, but it does have the folk museum with its memorable collection of barbed wire among other rural treasures, and, as it happens, the old school building. The Koppio building is identical with the demountable at Yallunda Flat - which I believe was later sent to needier parts further north - and from the surviving school records, evidently comparable with Yallunda Flat in almost every other respect, except that a curious remoteness and the baby boom of the 1950s kept the Koppio school open much longer. There were 29 children enrolled at Koppio in 1959, an all-time high.

In one-teacher schools, teachers had to keep numerous records as well as attendance books and their plans of work for frequent inspections - 11 on a list I saw for Koppio for 1905 - including a punishments book. Of special value historically are the teachers' journals and the twice-annual inspectors' reports (which teachers had to sign). The journals make delectable reading today, capturing, in Colin Thiele's words, 'the spirit of the times . . . the frustrations, humour, pathos, tragedy and trivia of the classroom, and of the world that enriched it' (*Grains of Mustard Seed*, p. 122). Likewise, the inspectors' reports offer assessments of work done and an overview, in this case of what was usually deemed 'a happy little school'.

As well as enrolment figures and the struggle to keep them up, Koppio teachers' journals record the main happenings of the school year: the annual school picnic, Arbor Day, Empire Day, Pioneers and Explorers Day, the Combined School Sports Day, the annual Christmas Tree, and, from 1945, Anzac Day, most with suitably shaped lessons: for instance on Empire Day in 1941 there were lessons on the growth and development of the British Empire and the flag and, after singing 'The Song of Australia' and 'God Save the King', a half holiday. Also recorded are nature study walks down by the creek, cleaning up the school garden, killing snakes, entries in the Yallunda Flat Show, several educational trips, and visitors such as the Methodist (now Uniting) Church minister for religious instruction, families and even, on one exalted occasion, the Minister for Education, who stressed the need for secondary education. As well, numerous events were held to raise funds during and after World War II – the Schools Patriotic Fund and then the Food For Britain Fund post war. It is amazing how much the tiny community raised for good causes by sales of school products, penny concerts, chop picnics (today they would be sausage sizzles) and euchre nights. At one dance they made over seven pounds, the equivalent of a good weekly wage in the city at that time. Listed also were the entries for the externally conducted final Quality Certificate examination, for which there was usually a candidate.

On 9 July 1946 the teacher's journal entry reads, 'The wireless arrived today and is very much admired'. A week later, the wireless having been installed by the parents who had raised the money for it, the children 'listened in' to their first wireless lesson. A couple of months later, bookshelves were installed. The parents, men as well as women, were untiring in their efforts and it is no wonder the inspectors were impressed.

The inspectors were seldom censorious, though some of the children were said to be plodders and others just scraped through the QC exam. The boy with a recorded mark of 541/800, who happened to be a cousin of mine, did comparatively well, and we were quite proud of him. Sometimes the inspectors worried that the children were not being taught enough history and geography and there are occasional complaints about limited vocabularies, but it was not until 1950 that a bad report appears. A supply teacher let things go, and the inspector found his work very disappointing. Among the many things noted was 'time of arrival at school' – the teacher said he had had to dry the spark plugs on his motorbike. He was transferred, perhaps to some drier place. It may be added that among the most poignant entries in the teachers' journal are those pertaining to late arrivals by pupils, who couldn't catch their horse or couldn't cross a creek. I believe them.

The area school

The school buses took us to an area school. First in Tasmania and then in South Australia, these combined schools were set up in country areas to provide all-in education suitable for rural children. Cummins Area School was one of the earlier ones, and by now there are about half a dozen across the Peninsula, maybe more, including one out in the middle of nowhere called Miltaburra Area School, off the Eyre Highway halfway between Wirrulla and Ceduna, not built until the 1980s because people couldn't agree on a location and now not surprisingly with a declining enrolment.

There's a lot to be said for area schools. Cummins particularly prided itself on its pioneering agricultural science course, introduced by David Floyd Smith, who went on to a distinguished academic career in the field. These days the course is available to both girls and boys, which was not the case in my time. Things have certainly changed in the country: I'm told one of the girls at Cummins won the Secondary School National Merino Shearing Competition in 2014.

The area schools also aimed to provide courses suitable for farmers' wives, such as domestic science and dressmaking. I always say I admire how well others did those courses but they were not for me. A valid criticism however is that it was not possible to qualify for university entrance as no languages were taught. This meant as things were then arranged that it was not possible for girls from area schools to become secondary school teachers. Three of us tried to teach ourselves Latin in the lunch hour but it was hard work, and recently the teacher who tried to help us out of hours told me that not much had been expected of me. One thing I do recall is that the art teacher Judith Clarkson introduced us to Aboriginal art. She also taught us about poetry in grade eight. If, when fate intervened and I moved to Adelaide, I had to repeat a year, it was not the fault of my teachers, it was the system, and that extra year was the making of me.

The challenge

Without the area school, who knows what kind of education I might have received. It is idle to speculate. One thing is certain, however: the school bus symbolised the end of an era. Together the area school and the school buses meant the end of the old one-teacher schools on Lower Eyre Peninsula, maybe as many as a dozen around us. Some, such as Mount Hill, did last until the 1980s, but they were very few. They cost too much, especially to such a poor state and, the truth is, they are no longer needed. Hank Nelson has described the national constituency of the one-teacher school very well as the school of the small farmers and those who serviced them. Nowadays farms are bigger and machines do a good deal of the work. Moreover, the regional economy has changed. It owes as much, if not more, to tourism and fishing as it does to farming. As elsewhere, the emphasis has shifted from the interior to the coast, where retirees now live in air-conditioned comfort, light-years away from the pioneering types recuperating over summer in shacks and tents as at Coffin Bay, and the wonderful old wooden jetties up and down both sides of the coast are valued more for their recreational than their economic significance. Meanwhile, the interior railway with its branch lines is now used only for goods and some of the villages that grew up along it are either deserted or worrying welfare sites. If the shape of regions has not really changed, their content has. As Nelson put it, 'Australia has been thinned'.[8]

In educational terms, a balanced appraisal may not be hard to arrive at, yet it is hard to deal with nostalgia, and perhaps something of importance has been lost. I would single out two aspects. In my view, many of today's educational institutions are far too large – for those

'The vehicle that closed the small schools.'

[*Grains of Mustard Seed*]

of you who recall Charles Dickens's great critique of mid-Victorian utilitarianism *Hard Times*, maybe Mr Gradgrind is on his way back. Of course the one-teacher schools were far too small, but the evidence is that many teachers had time to teach to the individual child. As well, it was wholesome for the children to experience continuous interaction with each other across the ages. The older children, especially the boys, could be very troublesome (and the older girls hoity-toity), nonetheless the engagement and responsibility of one for another we had of necessity on the school bus is not to be sneered at. As Colin Thiele puts it so well when recounting his own school days in a one-teacher school in the Barossa Valley, 'a school of that kind was really a family' (*Sun on the Stubble*, p. 25).

Another point of wider significance emerges here. In looking through the available records of Koppio School for the 1940s – a special period, to be sure – I was impressed by the commitment of the parents to the school and the way they valued its role in the community. As mentioned, the Koppio parents clubbed together to buy a radio set, and the dads built the receiver. Perhaps it is the same today. I hope so. But having said that, let's not lose sight of taxpayer support. A few years back we had the unseemly spectacle of a spokesman for the private schools defending the extent of their public funding by saying it was really the small country schools that cost so much. Of course they do, but they are needed. This country is too big and complicated for such nonsense.

The school bus revisited

Sometimes in histories of schooling we learn more about staff and buildings than we do about the students but I do not want that to be the case here. During my most recent trip back to Eyre Peninsula in October 2013, I and three of my fellow travellers on the Yallunda Flat school bus in the 1950s, Pat Green, Peter Blacker and Brian Laube, met at Pat's place in Port Lincoln to recall as many of the children who travelled on the bus in the early 1950s as possible. Between the four of us, we came up with 24 names – which seems a lot of children to have fit into the back of an enclosed utility, even counting the two seated up front with Mr Durdin, however the children were mostly under 14 years of age, and we managed to squeeze in as we went along.

We discovered from the morning's talk that there were equal numbers of boys and girls on the bus at that time, 12 boys and 12 girls, and that all but one were from farms along the way. Although this was far from being a scientific survey, all the usual caveats came into play with such data – some had passed beyond recall, several had already died, and less was known about the occupations of girls (apart, presumably for most, from marriage and home duties).

Thus with occupations, six boys went on to become farmers, with a further two joining the skilled working class in the towns. More exotically, one became a male nurse in Adelaide and another (whom I was delighted to run into when later I launched a book about the history of the Yallunda Flat Show) a pilot. Most of the boys remained on the Peninsula, but with the girls the story seems to have been different, with almost half in white-collar occupations or married or both beyond the Peninsula. My sister Heather for example, a primary school teacher, married a then fellow teacher from Mount Gambier, where they now live.

It was with pleasure that I recalled my fellow travellers on the bus, but with some sadness too, due to the premature deaths of Pat Green's brother Trevor Laube, a handsome bird-loving farmer, and yodeller and rodeo rider Mavis Walter, also her husband Bob Hughes.

What I hoped to learn from 'revisiting the school bus' was more about the larger issue of continuity and change over past decades. Perhaps it was a quixotic idea, but I would like to think that it makes a warm ending to this sliver of educational history in rural Australia.

CHAPTER 5

'Farming is fun': A child's perspective

dogs and horses – games we played – a turning point

Mostly when we think of life on the land it is from an adult's perspective, and if we think of children our minds probably turn to issues of opportunity, for example education and sport. But as for how children themselves actually experienced life on the land and what they felt about it at the time, the evidence is slim indeed. Of one thing we may be sure, however: schooling took up far less of a farm child's time than work and play, even taking into account the additional time spent on travel, and, with regard to priorities, it seems unlikely that it would come out on top for many of them. Perhaps things had changed by the mid-20th century, but compulsory attendance over a full school year until age 14 was only slowly established in this country and allowances were made for farm children until at least the 1950s (and probably still are), for instance older boys were eligible for leave to help with the harvest at year's end. In reality, for most children, being home on the farm was more fun than school.

In *Farming is Fun*, published in 1952, accountant A. Bertram Cox described his attempt to set up a hobby farm in the Adelaide foothills in the 1940s. Alas, it was a debacle. The book's title was ironic. No matter what he tried – and he tried most things, from fat lambs to cherries and olives – in the long run nothing really worked, due largely it seems to inexperience, insufficient acreage and the market, not to mention water, weeds and pests. 'We had our moments', Cox reflected, but by and large it was 'a harrowing experience'. To this, the old farmers who read his book nodded sagely and stuck to their guns, as did my father, who, like so many others, was about to reap the benefits of 'the wool boom'.

For us children, by that time life on the land was very different from that experienced by Cox, at least if my experience of a mixed cereals/sheep farm of some 800 hectares at Yallunda Flat is any guide. Certainly there was never any cash floating about, but that was probably due to the rhythm of farm income as much as anything and,

Farming is Fun **by A. Bertram Cox, Rigby, 1952.**

while the farm at Yallunda Flat was located in a comparatively well-watered area, there was probably not much regional variation in the pace and character of farm work by then.

We children had our own perspectives. Of course farming was not all fun, what with the relentless schedule of farm work and its seasonal variations to be maintained, usually with our help. Even so, for us the categories of work and play often overlapped in pleasurable ways, as with horse riding, and by that time very few of a farm child's jobs were downright disagreeable, although stone picking in newly cleared paddocks is one which springs to mind and, for girls, endless housework. Providing the weather was right, many jobs could be quite enjoyable, for instance picking peas in season and moving the sheep about. So, for the most part – but I must return to this aspect – was helping with the burning off of stubble and recent scrub clearings, usually done in the later, cooler, part of the day.

These days the problem of attracting young people to life on the land is very real. I was astounded recently to read in an account of a campaign to encourage the young back to the land, a list of challenges and tasks they might expect to face that included collecting eggs! Well, how times must have changed. In my day collecting the eggs was the littlest's job, and when it came to my turn to collect the eggs, I didn't at all mind checking the hens' nests when I got home from school, and looking for new ones. The black Orpingtons we mainly had liked to move around from time to time, even onto the thatched rooves that still covered the older sheds.

Not so enjoyable was my other after-school task, collecting the morning's wood, as we called the kindling needed to start the wood fires still basic to farm kitchens. In theory, finding kindling should not have been very onerous, but even for those of us in better-wooded country, supplies of fallen leaves and sticks were often limited. To collect an armful could be a challenge, and carrying it all back in jagged bundles to the house was hard on sensitive skin.

A related task pertained to the wood heap. Small bits of the stumps were needed to sustain the kitchen fires, and larger ones for maintaining open hearths for warmth in the winter. First, however, the stumps had to be picked from the paddocks and deposited in heaps, usually for convenience located near the kitchen. There they were chopped into usable sizes. Happily, the mallee trees of the region had large, multi-faceted stumps, easily chopped through. Mainly the men were supposed to do this job, but it was quite normal for women too, and even children. I did so myself from time to time. It helped you grow strong and keep fit, they said. Not until gas cylinders and electric stoves replaced the old wood stoves and open grates, which happened well after I'd left the farm and was a protracted development, did the work involved in maintaining them become a thing of the past for everyone, children, women, and men all. Meanwhile, the old ways persisted and domestic lighting remained a matter of candles and kerosene lamps, and maybe a torch to guide one to the outdoor lavatory at night.

The task everyone found most trying was undoubtedly milking cows. Nowadays farming households probably buy their milk refrigerated in plastic containers or cartons from a shop. Fifty or sixty years ago most mixed farms carried a few cows for domestic purposes, and in due course everyone took their turn at milking them. My turn came aged about eleven, at which time I recall we had some four or five Jersey and Guernsey milkers, my favourite being the most amiable, Maisie by name. Also memorable was ginger-coated

Daisy, who was inclined to toss her head and kick up when irritated.

Milking the cows was a demanding process. The cows had to be brought in from the paddocks ('getting the cows in' was a task thought suitable for younger children), bailed up in stalls in mucky cow yards and milked twice a day, the resultant buckets of milk then being carried off to the separator shed. There the milk was put through a separator, a hand-turned device dating from the 1880s which separated cream from the milk and had to be thoroughly washed every time it was used to ensure hygiene (which suddenly reminds me of the day in 1952 when I was about to wash the separator and my father appeared at the door to tell me my maternal grandmother had just died). Not being part of a large commercial enterprise, it was up to us to maintain the requisite standard of cleanliness.

Nor was separating the end of the drudgery. The skim milk was used to feed the calves and other farm animals, and cream that was not needed for domestic purposes was sent to the local butter factory, which resulted in handy pocket money for my older sisters – they, after all, did most of the work. But we did have plenty of fresh cream for ourselves: skimming cream off the 'top-of-the-milk' was only for those it pleased some of us to call 'townies', and thankfully there was as yet no such thing as school milk.

Remembering the cow yard conjures up, but only as in a faint blur, the image of another problematic farm animal: the pig. What bearing those pigs may have had on a child's work or play now lies beyond recall, except for two things: one, they seemed to have to be fed slops endlessly, and two, they often got out on Sunday mornings. Sunday was still a day of rest as far as possible. Even the cows were milked a bit later than usual. No doubt the pigs got hungry. But getting them back into the sty was no fun – despite their size they could move with surprising speed, and in ways hard for young children to anticipate. And so it was that pigs were dispensed with early on. Maybe it was just that they weren't a very profitable sideline for most farmers.

Dogs and horses

Of all the work-play overlaps for kids on farms, for me the most enjoyable were associated with dogs and horses, especially with Jock the kelpie and Mick the brumby.

The kelpie dog dates back to the 1870s, when selective breeding from among Scottish collies in New South Wales and Victoria, resulted in a superior working dog suited to local conditions. In appearance, the kelpie is plain but pleasing: sturdily built, smooth-coated and short haired, prick-eared, and predominantly dull red in colour. These days, many people's most vivid image of a kelpie probably comes from that wonderfully uplifting outback film *Red Dog* (2011), where a larger-than-life kelpie becomes a byword on the Pilbara for integrity and loyalty and, if not there already, part of Australian mythology.

An Australian Kelpie dog.

Our Jock was a typical kelpie, except perhaps he didn't have enough work to do, and was too often left tied up under the trees. But when he got to work, he put other dogs to shame. He could round up a mob of sheep and keep them moving in the required direction almost by himself. All one had to do was come along behind on a horse and make encouraging noises.

Maybe he was rather taciturn. I do recall trying to liven him up in a childish way and, what seemed a fun idea, to drop him in the sheep dip – an action I instantly regretted. Many country children had reason to take pleasure in the company of dogs as they went about their chores, and to this day I sometimes find myself missing old Jock. He wasn't flash but he was appealing in his own way: loyal, steady and a great worker.

Happily, it looks as though the working kelpie dog is here to stay. To the fear that the kelpie may die out, sheep farmers respond that they can't do without them, especially in rough country where motorbikes can't go.[1] They say that if they don't have kelpies they'll have to go back to collies, but 'kelpies have stronger personality, and don't mind a bit of challenge', and they can round up anything, even 'chooks and alpacas and goats'. Moreover there is now a Kelpie Council to defend the dog's interests. May it flourish: the kelpie's capacities certainly deserve to be cherished.

When exactly Mick the brumby came into our lives I can't recall or why, but it was probably a parental purchase in the later 1940s for us girls to ride around the locality and for the lighter farm work, such as rounding up sheep. At that time we still had a number of draught horses, and a semi-draught as well. The semi-draught was more versatile than the full draughts, but not so easy to handle.

A lot has been written about the horse in Australian history. Indeed, once you start looking into it, the literature on horses and horse-riding in this country is rather daunting, due to the vital role horses played in so many spheres of life and the economy until well into the 20th century, the glamour attached to 'the sport of kings', and the sheer size and variety of Australia's horse population over time. Of many references, I would highlight two as especially helpful here: the entry on horses in the *Wakefield Companion to South Australian History* (2001) and, in lieu of anything more local, Elwyne Mitchell's classic young people's novel *The Silver Brumby* (1958), set in the Snowy Mountains region.

Clydesdales on a mallee wheat farm.

[*Hauling the Load*]

Protected Coffin Bay brumbies.
[Coffin Bay Brumby Preservation Society Inc.]

By 1900, we learn from the general histories such as Ted Henzell's *Australian Agriculture* (CSIRO Publications, 2007), this country was incredibly well supplied with horses. One estimate is that in 1914 there were approximately 2.5 million horses Australia-wide and by 1920 there was one horse to almost every two people. The heyday of the horse came soon after, in the early 1920s, at which time it has been estimated there were approximately 270,000 horses in South Australia, some two-thirds of which were farm horses. As late as the 1940s horses did much of the work on the land and for children, more often than not with horses (like dogs), work became play.

In this context Mick was small beer. He was hardly fun, but he was always challenging. Swift of foot if he chose, sometimes he preferred to walk, in which case his young riders found that a good way to hurry him along was to lean forward on the saddle and crunch newspaper behind his ear. He was easily scared, and would sometimes shy at a shadow on the road. Fortunately, if taken by surprise it was not far for a young rider to fall.

Such behaviour is hardly surprising given the brumby's history. Like the kelpie, the brumby is not indigenous, but it dates back to colonial times, even further than the kelpie in fact, and, as with the word kelpie, the origins of the word brumby are uncertain. According to the *Australian Encyclopedia*, it may derive from a pioneer horse breeder called James Brumby, or possibly from a Queensland Aboriginal term for 'wild', or even from a creek there. Here it suffices to say that the brumby is simply an Australian word for a wild horse descended from runaway stock, this being a process that began very early and has since resulted in what is said to be the largest number of wild horses anywhere in the world. Estimates of present-day numbers in Australia vary but 400,000 seems a reasonable figure. These days, the brumby is mostly to be found in the north, in Queensland and the Northern Territory, also, and controversially, in the Australian Alps. Except around Lake Eyre and at Coffin Bay on the western tip of southern Eyre Peninsula, there are none in South Australia.

The Coffin Bay brumbies date back to the 1840s, when Timor ponies escaped from the tiny settlement at Port Lincoln, and the breed – if that's the word – was later strengthened by Coffin Bay pastoralist W.R. Mortlock. How many grew to be there is not known, but with closer settlement tensions increased, and by the early 20th century the brumbies had been removed eastward to the edge of the Coffin Bay National Park (finally gazetted in 1982). A century later they were further removed to a specified area on the edge of the township. This move seems to have proved a satisfactory compromise between the brumby-lovers and the environmentalists and enabled a smaller number of brumbies to flourish, with a Coffin Bay Brumby Preservation Society now established to maintain their position.

Our Mick was a Coffin Bay brumby dating from the 1930s. He was therefore partly domesticated. But not quite. It was that mix which made him so memorable.

Games we played

From a child's perspective, the most enjoyable aspects of life on the land in the early 20th century – that is, before mechanisation took over – were the games we made up about our lives and the plants and animals that shared those lives.

No doubt my experience was in some respects unrepresentative, since my favourite game was the solitary one, mentioned earlier, played at various points along Kooltatta Creek, the minor tributary of the Tod River which ran through our property. I spent hours on the job of ensuring that the water ran smoothly throughout the year. It now seems rather odd, but it did no harm and maybe some good, and it underlines the centrality of water in that part of the world.

Yabbying was a creek-related activity, as I also noted earlier. We didn't go yabbying very often, but the yabby is delicious and a good catch was worth the effort. Much is still to be learned about the yabby; however, these days in South Australia the state encourages yabby farming and there are now some 300 yabby farms set up there,

Mallee Bush Pea.
[*Wildflowers of Lower Eyre Peninsula*]

a handbook for would-be growers and a Growers' Association, with a branch at Coffin Bay.

Some of the most enjoyable activities were purely seasonal. In autumn there were wild mushrooms to be picked on the hillsides. Fresh wild mushrooms are probably a thing of the past, but to bring a basketful in to be cooked straight away and eaten as the evening meal was an unbeatable experience. They tasted nothing like today's commercially grown mushrooms, even the best and mildest of button mushrooms. Likewise, wildflowers were to be found in the scrub in spring. The orchid patch I cherished on one such hillside held small, brown native orchids – probably the fringed spider orchid common to Lower Eyre Peninsula, according to two modest but very informative booklets that have been produced documenting native flora of the area, *Wildflowers of Lower Eyre Peninsula* (first published in 1994, reprinted in 2001) and its companion booklet *Quieter Wildflowers of Lower Eyre Peninsula* (undated).

The temptation to retrieve other farm children's games from memory has to be resisted, if only for reasons of space, but one more absolutely must be included here. It was played all year round, and as mentioned in my recollections of school bus days, it was simply called 'little'. It was devised by one of the boys at our one-teacher school at Yallunda Flat, Bob Blacker, and, although considered a boys' game, it was absorbing for girls as well. I recalled this game for Hank Nelson's delightful book *With Its Hat about Its Ears: Recollections of the bush school* (p. 151), published by ABC Books in 1989, as follows:

> In the schoolroom girls were tops and in the yard boys ran things. Parents would lament that their boys were so unscholarly, and how they would regret it later in life, but the fact was that they were there to become small farmers, they wanted to be nothing but small farmers, and what we did in recess and at lunch time was play farms.
>
> We played farms endlessly. The game was called 'little'. It was an exact replica of what was going on in the farms of the community. And the boys ran that area of our lives.

The boys weren't particularly interested in academic work. All through my rural education the girls were scrupulous, interested, quiet and good. The boys were troublesome. At best they didn't have too many inkblots on their books and were quiet until allowed to get on with the real business of sport and farms.

'Little' was quite imaginative. Everything that came to hand was used to reproduce the farming season and life. Pine-cones in various stages were used for sheep, cattle and horses. Other bits and pieces scattered round were used to make roads and buildings. Paddocks were laid out. A good size farm at Yallunda Flat School was five feet by ten. Everything that went on there was supposed to reflect what went on in the wider society. The land was scratched into furrows. When it rained the land was turned over again. After harvest there was a burning-off in the surrounding stubble, and attempts were made to burn-off in the school. I blush to recall that I once set the schoolyard on fire. Fortunately it didn't go too far because stinkweed, which covered half the yard, is evergreen and unburnable. But everyone had to come and put it out.

The game was nomadic. Weeks would go by then someone would see better land down the yard, and slowly we would all shift. At times we would play other games. But the ruling game was 'little'.

I'm afraid there was another occasion when I overdid 'burning off'. I also played 'little' at home, and one Sunday morning, when no one else was there, the fire got away from me. Fortunately people were coming home from church and saw the smoke, and it was speedily extinguished. They arrived just as the flames approached the garden fence around the house. No one could bring themselves to speak about it until later, and I never tried 'burning off' again.

Maybe 'spotlighting' should be mentioned too. It certainly was a popular sport among young men at the time, but it was not until after my father's remarriage in 1950 brought a stepbrother into our lives and my sisters had boyfriends that it impinged on me. By now I can only recall participating on one occasion, and I still feel a bit squeamish about it, although driving about the paddocks on the back of a utility at night holding a spotlight while the men shot mainly at rabbits was undoubtedly exciting, and it probably predated the impact of myxomatosis on the region's rabbit population (the *myxoma* virus was introduced into Australia in 1950).

A turning point

I try to encapsulate life on the farm the 1940s and 1950s in the phrase *Mechanisation Takes Command*, the title of a classic work on the theme published by Swiss historian Sigfried Giedion in 1948. Thinking about the imaginative experiences of farm children is a reminder that, before the coming of the tractor, the truck, and the motorbike, neither animals nor people were there for decorative purposes. One way or another, and according to their capacities, they were there to work, to earn a living. The draught horse is the most obvious example of that imperative, and conspicuously so in places like Eyre Peninsula, where, on the one hand, bullocks were still needed for clearing in the early 20th century, and on the other, geography, that is to say flat lands and ready access to the sea, enabled the longer use of the much cheaper draught horse.

Somehow the draught horse represented the adult world: all work and no play. Childhood recall dredges up little more than the sight of them in stables, and a memory of taking tea out to the men in the paddocks during cropping. By the early 1940s it was almost all over for the draught horse on Eyre Peninsula. Learning to drive a tractor became the great challenge for the young, especially for boys but, depending on circumstances and temperament, for girls too.

It seems inevitable that there are limits to what personal memories can offer to the larger picture. For one thing there's a skew in this narrative, in that there were no boys in our family, so we girls did more than usual of the outdoor work. Other farm girls probably did more housework in those early years, when we mostly had housekeepers, and I, being the youngest, didn't really learn to cook or sew, though we all did quite a bit of housework, such as washing up, sweeping floors and making the beds. Moreover, life on the farm had undoubtedly become somewhat easier by the 1950s, and the experiences recounted here occurred on the cusp of change, which means there is a danger of overdoing the fun side of things. It seems only right then to conclude with the draught horse. For a century or more the draught horse was the quintessential farm animal, a noble creature that epitomised hard work, of the kind that many children of earlier times knew only too well. Perspective matters.

CHAPTER 6

'We plough the fields and scatter': Church and community

the churches – the community – changing perspectives – a note on memorials

The title quotation, 'We plough the fields and scatter', is from the opening line of a popular harvest thanksgiving hymn dating back to a German poem of late 18th century and first translated in English in 1861.

We plough the fields, and scatter
The good seed on the land;
But it is fed and watered
By God's almighty hand;
He sends the snow in winter,
The warmth to swell the grain,
The breezes, and the sunshine,
And soft refreshing rain.

Chorus

All good gifts around us
Are sent from heaven above;
Then thank the Lord, O thank the Lord,
For all His love.

'He sends the snow in winter' aside, its relevance to predominantly farming communities in a region of recent European settlement such as Eyre Peninsula will be obvious. The hymn was still being sung in churches in the 1950s.[1]

The churches

How many churches were built on Eyre Peninsula between the late 1840s and 1960 it is impossible to say, especially as so many have now been moved, fallen into disrepair, or disappeared completely. But of one thing we may be sure: no community was at some stage or another without at least one. Moreover, except for missions to Aboriginal groups, and as with schools, it was usually the settlers themselves who took the initiative in setting them up. Sometimes the churches they built were impressive stone constructs, for example St Augustine's and St Canute's, the Anglican and Catholic churches of Streaky Bay on the upper west coast, an area with a long pastoral history. Both date from 1912. But even at Streaky Bay the churches had modest beginnings, and in many places they made do with corrugated iron. Later, and well into the 20th century, some denominations sent home missioners to the region, usually to the sparsely settled inland. For various reasons, not least unsuitable candidates, such centrist initiatives were all too often disappointing.

My first 'church' was Anglican, up Wudinna way, in the late 1940s at Pygery. Even then, Pygery was little more than a railway siding in an area of closer settlement dating back at most two generations, and the tiny congregation met in a corrugated iron hall (which no longer exists) monthly, if I recall correctly. More vivid is the memory of a light aeroplane landing in the front paddock of my maternal grandmother's

A Bush Church Aid plane at Mount Elba, c. 1944.
[The Neil Follett Collection p1234–0259]

nearby farm. It was a Bush Church Aid plane, bringing much-needed medical assistance from the organisation's regional base at Ceduna. Bush Church Aid, an Anglican Home Mission Society initiative, was founded in Sydney in 1921, and its aerial medical service operated throughout much of the far western interior from the late 1930s to 1968, when it was integrated with the Reverend John Flynn's Royal Flying Doctor Service, which dates from 1928.[2]

My second church was another little corrugated iron building down south, this one purpose-built at Yallunda Flat on the western edge of a Methodist circuit based at Tumby Bay. At that time Sunday services were held fortnightly at 11 am, and sometimes as many as 30 people turned up, including, with luck, someone who could play

After the service at the Methodist Church at Yallunda Flat, c. late 1950s. [*Gum Trees and Gullies*]

the pedal organ. The Roes always went, and the then preacher, the Rev. Stanley Forth, usually came to lunch afterwards (always a mutton roast, left to cook in the oven of a wood stove while we were at church). Afterwards Mr Forth would go on to an afternoon service up the road, and we went off to tennis or basketball practice – though this could not be mentioned since Sunday was supposed to be a day of rest.[3]

Churchgoing was a community activity, and what happened during the hour-long service made little if any perceptible impact on the young, at least not on me. There was no Sunday School for us. We just had to sit still and stay quiet during the service and those who couldn't or wouldn't were sent outside. It is probably a myth that the noisy ones were tied up under the trees. Afterwards the grown-ups stood around talking and the children ran about until it was time for lunch. At home, we always said grace before meals. There was an everyday one which we children took it in turns to say, 'Bless this food of which we take, to do us good for Jesus' sake', and a special one for

Sundays, said by our father, 'Be present at our table Lord/Be here and everywhere adored/These mercies bless/and grant that we/May feast in Paradise with Thee'. It was said, not entirely as a joke, that grace gave everyone an equal start on the food. As well, we had structured Bible readings prepared by Scripture Union at home in the evenings. But churchgoing was a sociable occurrence, a sign of belonging and of respectability. That there might be more to it, I vaguely realised from the only sermon I can recall from those distant days – considerable stress was laid on sermons by the Methodists. It was a pre-Christmas sermon, something about 'the green light', which was possibly a reference to a novel of that name by popular American writer Lloyd Douglas, who died in 1951.

Something more substantial may have seeped through, nonetheless. Sent to the city to complete secondary schooling, I continued going to church (Pirie Street Methodist). And although by then Methodist services seemed dull and dreary, there must have been some genuine awareness. My father had read popular works such as H.V. Morton's *In the Steps of the Master* (1934), and one of my earliest attempts at writing, a review of *The Greatest Story Ever Told* (1949), was published in the Cummins Area School Magazine in 1953 and predates my move to Adelaide. Later my interest in religious topics increased, partly no doubt due to my stepmother, whose first husband had been a clergyman. When I discovered that she had given his books to the Anglican rector in Port Lincoln, I took it upon myself to call at the rectory to ask if I could borrow some of them. The books in question were by Englishman Geoffrey Studdert-Kennedy, an Anglican cleric and poet better known during World War I as 'Woodbine Willie'. Studdert-Kennedy (1883–1929) was a pacifist and Christian socialist.

Anglicanism was not the largest denomination on Eyre Peninsula, but it was one of the oldest, with 'presence' and some substantial accomplishments, most notably Poonindie Mission, north of Port Lincoln. The Poonindie Mission, established as early as 1850 by an Anglican clergyman, Matthew Hale – later Bishop of Perth – was the first Aboriginal mission on the Peninsula, and, so its historians Peggy Brock and Doreen Kartinyeri tell us, in its mid-Victorian heyday rather like 'a holy village'. Closed down in 1894 due, apparently, to pressure from land-hungry small farmers, the mission lands have now been returned to Aboriginal people. Some buildings have survived, including the original and still functional 'church with a chimney'. We drove by them often, but the mission was something of a mystery to me. The less said the better, presumably.

My friend Baiba Berzins at 'the church with a chimney', 2013.

The Reverend Alexander Macintosh, whose books I was after that day in Port Lincoln, served in the Anglican Diocese of Willochra, which takes in most of the west and the north of South Australia. The Rev. Macintosh was trained on the Isle of Man and died shortly after arriving on Eyre Peninsula. Like the Adelaide diocese from which it was carved in 1915, Willochra had a High Church flavour – which perhaps explains why Anglicanism scarcely impinged on farmers' daughters like me. But there are some good stories embedded in its history, and some colourful figures. One such was the Reverend George Wilfred Scholefield, the Anglo-Catholic assistant priest at the Cummins-Minnipa Mission from 1930 to 1935, whose field stretched some 120 miles north from Cummins to Minnipa. Scholefield, a man remembered for repaying hospitality with vegetables he had grown himself, went on to serve at Port Pirie until 1956, and in later life recorded his mainly happy experiences of the Cummins-Minnipa Mission. That was well before my time, but he probably did minister to some of my Heath relatives at Pygery, and he married my parents at Wudinna on Wednesday, 26 April 1933.[4]

There were also weekly Religious Instruction classes in South Australian schools by the 1940s. 'RI' was scarcely memorable, except that at one stage my class at Cummins was taken by the Lutheran minister who I now realise spoke with a German accent. This experience should perhaps have alerted me to the wider regional importance of Lutheranism but of this I was basically oblivious, and there is a reason. The real strength of Lutheranism lay to the north. The first Lutherans came across the Gulf to Cowell from the 1860s onwards as the land to the east, in the Barossa and on Yorke Peninsula, filled up. Lutheranism spread westward towards Ceduna and beyond, its adherents establishing numerous small churches along the way, such as the Bethlehem Lutheran Church near Denial Bay, west of Ceduna, as early as 1896. Southward expansion came later. It is probably relevant too that on Eyre Peninsula, as elsewhere in South Australia, services were conducted in German until the 1930s. Lutheran history is a rather complicated subject, due to theological divisions not fully overcome until the 1960s, but it seems the then main branch, the United Evangelical Lutheran Church of Australia (the UELCA), became securely based on the Peninsula.[5]

The farthest reach of Lutheranism was not solely due to local initiative. Like other denominations, urban Lutherans struggled to support home missioners and, in South Australia, missions to Aboriginal groups. On Eyre Peninsula their main initiative was Koonibba, a mission north-west of Ceduna, founded in 1898 and run by the church until 1963 when it was taken over by the state. Koonibba is now an Aboriginal settlement with enduring links to the Lutheran Church. Like Poonindie, the outcomes have been mixed. Unlike Poonindie, to which young people from all over the colony were sent, Koonibba served local and displaced inland peoples. Much later, and even further west, the Lutheran-run Yalata mission served a similar purpose under even more dire circumstances, with Aboriginal people from the interior being relocated there in 1952 due to British atomic testing at Maralinga in the far north-west of South Australia, which went on until 1963.[6] Lutheran responsibility lasted a little over two decades: the Aboriginal community took control of the reserve in July 1975.[7]

As for Catholicism, now somewhat surprisingly the largest denomination in South Australia, it was a minority presence on Eyre

Lutheran Church at Koonibba.

Peninsula, with churches on the edge of small towns and services in Latin to which schoolgirls like me were not obliged – or equipped – to pay attention. However, as with Anglicanism, it had some 'presence' in the larger towns, especially Port Lincoln, where the imposing St Mary of the Angels and the adjacent convent-cum-school dating back to the 1860s stand on the southern rise. The first nuns were 'Brown Joeys', members of St Mary MacKillop's order, but their tenure was short-lived; the last nun, a member of the succeeding 'Black Joeys' at St Mary's compound, retired in 2004.

There is a touch of romance to the history of Catholicism on Eyre Peninsula too, in that for much of the 19th century one Father had to minister to the entire west coast. Long tours of duty and irregular ministrations under rough circumstance were quite normal in the

St Mary of the Angels Catholic Church in Port Lincoln.

early days, as were colourful clerics, such as Danish-born Friar Pedar Jorgensen (resident Port Lincoln, 1894–1916). He administered the sacraments in parlours, halls, shops, woolsheds, even in tents and under trees. On one trip out west, Jorgensen was about to return from Fowlers Bay when he heard of four Catholics working further out on the Dog Fence, so he borrowed fresh horses and set off to celebrate mass with them 'under the mallee bushes'. On a later trip through the Peninsula, Bishop Norton covered 1000 miles and administered 250 baptisms and confirmations. Sometimes more adults than children were confirmed.[8]

Probably there was an element of inter-faith rivalry in all this, and a sectarian strand too – as I recall, Catholics were usually referred to as 'Roman Catholics' (with the emphasis on 'Roman') and in popular parlance 'the Micks' (which of course meant Irish), but I have yet to see it documented.

It is not my main purpose of this chapter to list all the various denominations on Eyre Peninsula but, as is probably apparent by now, the most popular of them all has yet to be considered; Methodism (now part of the Uniting Church). The Methodist system of preaching circuits enabled regular services – by lay as well as ordained preachers – in most places. Like Yallunda Flat, there were also fortnightly services in the Cummins district, where the first Methodist church opened as early as 1912, and a similar sequence of services was established at the numerous preaching places on northern Eyre Peninsula: at Streaky Bay, Ceduna, and beyond, as graphically detailed in *Faith on the Western Front* (1977). Even in the era when it was compulsory to answer the religion question in the national census, Methodism performed almost as strongly as the Church of England in South Australia, with 100,402 ticking Methodism compared to Anglicanism's record of 113,781 in 1911, and the former is said to have been stronger in the country than the city. By 1960, when Methodism peaked on Eyre Peninsula, it could boast 36 churches and 29 preaching places.[9]

Surprisingly – perhaps impressively would be a better word – an effort seems to have been made to minister to their adherents by or on behalf of practically every known denomination, despite small populations and the unending expense. One denomination that succeeded in a minor way was the Church of Christ, an Anglo-American protestant denomination dating from the early 19th century, with five churches at Port Lincoln, Tumby Bay, Ungarra, Whyalla, and Tjilgamooda, Ceduna, an Aboriginal community church. A contrasting example would seem to be Presbyterianism. A missionary established churches on the lower west coast before World War I, and a church was built at Cummins at that time, but none appear to have survived. At best the Presbyterians gained a temporary toehold. Meanwhile, some other smaller denominations such as the Baptists were securely established on the eastern coast, with churches at Port Lincoln and Whyalla, and even reached a few places up the west coast, such as Chandada, where two Sisters worked in the 1940s, although they seldom went far into the interior. In any event, such gaps hardly mattered to people in the early days. They simply went along to whatever services were available or, like the Moss family of Darke Peak, travelled to the nearest town where Mass was being celebrated that day, whether at Cleve, Lock or Kimba. If truth be told, even in this thinly settled and predominantly rural region, by the early 20th century the proportions attending services were probably similar to those of the state as a whole in most instances.

The community

In his 1985 history of Methodism in South Australia, *This Side of Heaven*, Arnold Hunt notes that religion in agricultural communities across the world have over the centuries spawned a variety of ceremonies associated with the gathering of the harvest (p. 161). Harvest festivals, he tells us, became popular from about the 1860s, and were universally observed in the Methodist church in South Australia, even in bad years. If I ask myself what services in that tiny church at Yallunda Flat so long ago were actually memorable, the first to spring to mind would be the annual harvest thanksgiving. I think of it as being in late November/early December. At this service, the altar and communion table would be decorated with produce, bundles of wheat and barley, fruit and vegetables, flowers, maybe even eggs. It was at harvest thanksgiving that we sang 'We plough the fields and scatter/ The good seed on the land'. According to Hunt, the produce was often sold after the service, though I do not recall this. There wasn't much at Yallunda Flat that was saleable anyway.

This observance leads on to other church ceremonies integral to community life and wellbeing. Congregations rallied for church services at Christmas and Easter and, until at least the 1960s, churches underwrote the life cycle. Adherents' babies were baptised. Some denominations required that children be confirmed. Marriages should be properly conducted. So should burials. Of course, these ceremonies were not compulsory, and some people did not observe them; in any case, the registrations were underpinned by the state. However, perhaps more than in the city, such ceremonies brought people together with a sense of purpose, and they represented respectability and stability. For healthy communities, there had to be churches and churchmen, regardless of denominational niceties and the financial problems that beset them all, and this was especially so in new and disrupted communities.

There is a further dimension to 'church and community': the cultural dimension. This dimension is often overlooked and has not been a part of the historian's lexicon for some time, but its relevance is the more obvious in new and distant communities. I've mentioned pedal organs and hymn singing; though pianos were popular from the days of first settlement, an organ was a grander instrument than most could afford at home, and an opportunity for everyone to sing was provided by the hymns. A similar point could be made about Bibles, prayer books and edited selections of devotional readings in communities where reading matter was limited. Perhaps most importantly for people who had few other outings and opportunities, churchgoing was an enjoyable social and cultural event – a time to chat under the trees after services and, for women at least, an opportunity to wear one's best clothes. For Catholic Evelyn Nelson in her aptly named memoir *Getting By* (2000), churchgoing was 'a fashion parade almost' (pp. 33–34). By filling psychological needs later catered for by secular means and/or secularised forms of authority, such as marriage celebrants and funeral parlours, the communal wellbeing was enhanced. 'Tin-kettlings' of newlyweds, the noisy banging of pots and pans to celebrate a wedding, one of which I recall, are not strictly speaking relevant, but they do belong somewhere nearby, being an attenuated version of the ancient European ritual of charivari.

Maybe material wellbeing was also a religious consideration. If we prayed for rain I do not recall it, but in earlier times and the drier parts they certainly did. Hunt mentions Wesleyan recourse to prayer in 1886, when rain fell after a 'Day of Humiliation and Prayer'. In the 1885–1887 diaries of a colonial teenager, *Stagg of Tarcowie* (Lutheran Publishing House, 1973), it is recorded that after prayers for rain on one Palm Sunday, the drought broke. These days most farmers depend on the weather bureau and the media.

Changing perspectives

To establish churches and preaching places in remote areas was one thing; to maintain them has been another. Even to Methodism, and no doubt other denominations, the west coast was 'its severest challenge' (Hunt). Today many of those smaller rural and regional churches established a century or so ago have been moved, closed down or demolished, as has happened to that little tin church at Yallunda Flat with which I began. At Sheringa, south of Elliston, a place now better known for historic stone fences and on-going racial tension, the Anglican church struggles to survive, and the historic Anglican Church of the Epiphany at Lipson inland from Tumby Bay does so in association with the Uniting Church.[10] Even the most securely established churches in South Australia's larger towns have fewer functions and smaller congregations by now. The coming of new features, such as the Greek Orthodox churches in fishing communities and post-1960s forms of fundamentalism, remain to be studied, as does the religio-political underbelly of rural life: apparently the Catholic rural movement launched by B.A. Santamaria in Melbourne in the 1940s did comparatively well on Eyre Peninsula, and the later League of Rights gained a following in the 1970s.

Much has been written about the decreasing strength and significance of churches across the 20th century, including in rural Australia, but, apart from Ian Breward in his *History of the Australian Churches* (1993), few have noticed rural/urban variations in levels of commitment over time, or the variations in perspective. In rural Australia, Breward writes, 'despite economic stringency [in the 1890s] there was often strong community feeling' (p. 92). This localism and sense of identity is probably still quite strong. Although it is clear from statistics that traditional churchgoing has everywhere greatly declined since the 1960s, a country town without churches and churchgoers would still be anomalous.

By way of closure, I offer a perspective on the changing position of churches in society. As Doreen Rosman observed in her fine study *The Evolution of the English Churches* (Cambridge, 2003), 'Men and women born in the later 19th and early 20th centuries were probably more exposed to religious teaching than any previous generation' (p. 296). This surely applied to South Australians, at least until the great cultural watershed that we call the 1960s.

However, churchgoers have probably changed too. A glimpse of changing perspectives comes with the celebration of 100 years of the Anglican church at Tumby Bay, St Margaret's, in 2008. An ornament of the Diocese of Willochra thanks to the early beneficence of the once dominant pastoral Mortlock family, St Margaret's now has a

Church of Saint Margaret at Tumby Bay.

modest though committed adherence. Interestingly, at its centenary celebrations, an area was set aside in the church grounds for the reception of adherents' ashes. The remains of the Reverend Macintosh and his wife (later my stepmother) have been buried together in the local cemetery. These days, their ashes could be placed side by side in the grounds of the church that brought them to South Australia in the late 1940s, and thus into my story.[11]

A note on memorials

It may surprise the reader to find that this account of 'church and community' ends with a brief note on war and other memorials. However, I can recall at least two memorials at churches on the Peninsula. Both are in the Tumby Bay Methodist/Uniting Church circuit, the circuit closest to my own experience, and both are still there. At Yallunda Flat, there is a war memorial between what was then the shop and a Methodist church that dates back to 1921. Unusually, it is a pine plantation that in my day had a plaque at the base of each tree commemorating those who were killed in action or returned safely, 22 in all. Now, when it seems there are fewer trees, there is a single freestanding list of names.[12] More recently, a Pioneer Women's Memorial was established on the grounds of the Stokes church. It commemorates the women who established homes in the district between the 1860s and the 1900s, and in 2013 it celebrated its 50th anniversary.

Probably the locations of these memorials are due to the availability of land at the time. But the association of such memorials with church and community is striking; and our thinking about them has been transformed in recent times, especially by Ken Inglis's *Sacred*

The Yallunda Flat Memorial Park pine plantation.

The Stokes Pioneer Women's Memorial.

Places: War memorials in the Australian Landscape, published in 1998, and by new approaches to women's history dating back to the 1970s. These days it is quite common to regard war memorials as 'sacred sites' and to think of Anzac Day as the high point in a 'secular religion', while the memorial to pioneer women at Stokes was unveiled on Mother's Day, 12 May 1963, a Sunday. I feel sure more such linkages will come to light during the centenary of World War I and with the passage of time.

CHAPTER 7

'I danced for the Queen': Exuberance and otherwise in regional history since the 1950s

the royal visit – some wider considerations – a new regionalism?

The royal visit

At 2.20 pm on Saturday, 20 March 1954, the plane bearing the young Queen Elizabeth II and her consort, HRH Prince Philip, was scheduled to touch down at Port Lincoln aerodrome, which had a spanking new terminal for the occasion. The plane was a little late arriving from Whyalla, where the royal couple had spent the morning, but the 15,000 strong crowd, mostly assembled along the main street, Tasman Terrace, and at the nearby Centennial Oval, waited in good humour. Happily, although it was an overcast day, there was a refreshing westerly breeze, and the sun came out briefly as the royal entourage drove southwards along the shores of Boston Bay towards the city, escorted by a flotilla of sailing boats with speed boats zipping in and out, and the royal cars, brought specially from Adelaide, picked up speed en route, to arrive more or less on time for the official reception at Civic Hall at the centre of town. The visit was timed to last a little under two hours, and the royal plane was able to leave for Adelaide at 4.15 pm, as scheduled.[1]

The royal visit of 20 March 1954 was undoubtedly the biggest event ever to be hosted by the regional city in its century-plus years.

The local authorities did not fail to meet the challenge presented, nor the people, who came from as far as Eucla, to see for themselves the first ruling monarch ever to set foot on Australian soil. Preparations, overseen by the mayor of Port Lincoln, Mr W.A. Trigg, and others, had been in train for months, with a full dress rehearsal under the eye of the state royal tour marshal the week before, and the press played an important part in preparing people and place for the royal presence, publicising for example the correct ways of decorating shops in the main street and explaining where flags could be placed on one's car (only the royal car could attach a flag at the top of the car hood, but we could fly one from the bonnet cap). By this stage of the tour it was not apparently deemed necessary to advise the populaces on manners, as was the case in Melbourne, though we were urged to show the royal couple that we were really pleased to see them – and not to throw anything at the cars in the royal progress, nor to litter the streets, and at that time Australian women could curtsey as to the manner born, though little girls were sometimes overcome, as happened in Mount Gambier, when the Queen reportedly whispered to 6-year-old Margaret Mary Moles; 'Bend your knee, dear'. Afterwards, Sergeant Ridge, officer-in-charge of Port Lincoln Police Station, said that the crowds had been very well behaved throughout.[2]

Apart from an anxious moment the preceding day, when the bound illuminated address to be presented to the Queen did not arrive from Adelaide until the late plane, it all went like clockwork. There was to be a change of cars at an undisclosed point, and the royal progress began when the entourage passed under a 30-foot-high welcome arch decorated with ferns and flowers by the CWA, located at (I think) Baudin Place. When the roar of speed boats indicated that the royal cars were approaching the city, the hush which had fallen over the waiting crowds changed to cheers, as the open car bearing the young Queen and her handsome consort travelled slowly to Civic Hall, where they alighted and went inside. Mayor Trigg, wearing a freshly minted mayoral Chain of Office, then welcomed the Queen to Port Lincoln from the balcony of Civic Hall. In his brief address of welcome, he emphasised the progress of a pioneering community, its association with Lincolnshire and explorer Matthew Flinders, and its loyalty to the crown, stating in conclusion:

> 'On this memorable occasion we desire to express to Your Majesty, in person, our loyalty, devotion and affectionate attachment to Your Person and the Throne. We are proud to say that our loyalty to the British Empire is true, steadfast, and unquestioned, and our earnest prayer is for its prosperity and progress for many years under your peaceable reign.'[3]

In response the Queen paid tribute to the pioneering ethos and the explorers, and expressed faith in the future of Eyre Peninsula:

> 'The successes which have been achieved here are due in no small measure to the pioneering spirit and the hard work of your men and women. They in their turn must have been encouraged by the endurance and tenacity of purpose of Edward John Eyre. I am sure that this corner of your State is destined to play an increasing part in the development of South Australia and the Commonwealth.'[4]

The Queen was said to look 'almost solemn', but when the official party retired to the mayoral chambers, decorated with gold-tinted dahlias and roses, she turned to wave to the crowd below and, in the words of the *Port Lincoln Times*, on whose excellent reportage this account is drawing, 'flashed them a warm, glowing smile'. (Unlike some writers on royal visits elsewhere, the report didn't discuss rules precluding mention by the press of the location of the royal toilets, presumably in the mayoral chambers; there were many such rules to protect the dignity of the monarchy from, for example, commercial exploitation.)

After the welcome and a brief further progress around the southern streets of the city, the royal party reached Centennial Oval, where they witnessed a children's display. It seems to be agreed that this was the highlight of the Queen's visit to Port Lincoln. Actually, children's displays were a program highlight everywhere, and the Queen who, as was pointed out many times, was herself the mother of two young children – appeared to enjoy them. The first display had been in Sydney, where 150,000 schoolchildren rallied at four locations to greet her soon after her arrival in Australia on the royal yacht *Gothic* from New Zealand some six weeks earlier (3 February), and a few days after she returned to Adelaide from the Whyalla–Port Lincoln trip, on the afternoon of 23 March, approaching 100,000 schoolchildren were assembled at the Wayville Oval to present a carefully devised program of band music, physical education formations, musical movements and dances (of the wattle blossom and of the hoops), and tableaux. These days we pay big money to entrepreneurs for comparable public spectacles, whereas 60 years ago teachers did most of the work, but that is by the by. What the Queen said to the children on these occasions I have not sought to ascertain, but there can hardly be an older person in Australia without some recollection of her, however fleeting.[5]

On the oval at Port Lincoln, the children formed a floral fan to welcome their royal highnesses. The fan was designed by Miss Josephine West, senior teacher at Port Lincoln Primary School, as a display of regional wildflowers and some 900 children from schools of Lower Eyre Peninsula participated, 16 schools in all, with another 2500 children who came from 55 schools further out, flanking the display. The boys, all in white, sat cross-legged within an outline of Lower Eyre Peninsula drawn on the oval, to form the ribs of the fan, and the girls were arranged in panels in between, according to school. The girls were also arranged horizontally according to height in bands of wildflowers across the fan, with the tallest girls at the back as Sturt's Desert Peas, and bands of Templetonia, wild lilacs, pink and blue orchids, wattle, gumnuts and billy buttons in descending order, towards the bottom of the fan and the royal dais. According to a letter from Miss West in my possession, written much later, the girls' dresses were made of silk-like material donated by the Education Department – I would have said light hessian myself – and the costumes were dyed appropriate colours, including the shoes and socks, and the head gear, which was based on babies' bonnets with material or *papier mâché* additions, all made by the mothers under local guidance in accordance with designs by Mrs G.L. Reade of Lockleys.[6] The overall effect was doubtless quite something, as in the representation of the desert pea, with its brilliant red flower and black boss, which the Queen is said to have identified immediately, having seen the flowers at Broken Hill two days earlier, en route to South Australia from Brisbane. The desert pea is of course the South Australian floral emblem. Perhaps this is the place to confess what is doubtless already obvious, that I was in the back row that day. I was what was called a big girl, and my memory of it is hazy, not to say a bit woozy, but yes, I danced for the queen.

According to the *Port Lincoln Times*, we began the display from the map and danced gracefully to our positions on the fan and, after a change of music, swayed from side to side as though stirred by a gentle breeze, changing motions when the music changed again to a polka, at which point the movements became more dance-like and the fan became 'a massive sea of colour'. The display, it comes as a surprise to find, lasted a mere five minutes, and ended with a bow to the Queen and the Duke. It was reported that they were delighted, and joined in the enthusiastic applause of some 7000 parents and onlookers. They then descended from the dais, the Queen carrying a bouquet presented by the young Ruth Trigg, for a final round of the oval and departure for the aerodrome. Journalists following the royal tour said the display was easily as good as anything seen so far, and that they had never seen the Queen in a happier mood.[7]

Another group to put its best foot forward were the ex-servicemen who lined the streets and policed the car parks, and their comrades in the Citizens Military Force (CMF), who carried the Queen's Colours. As well, special seating was allocated at the Civic Hall to war widows and disabled servicemen. It is an often overlooked fact that, from the monarchy's point of view, the main purpose of the tour, apart from cementing loyalty to the Crown, was to thank the Commonwealth for its contribution to victory in World War II. Political leaders in Britain and Australia who had envisaged the tour as early as 1948, had more mundane links in mind, but the monarch is Head of the Armed Forces, and in most places the first thing the Queen did was lay a wreath at the war memorial. Unless I have missed something this does not seem to have happened in Port Lincoln. Perhaps she paused before the roll honouring the men who fought in World War I situated in the Civic

Hall. The memorial to be seen on the lawns at Port Lincoln honours all those who fought in wars from the Boer War to the Vietnam War but was established quite recently, probably in the last decade.[8]

In an article in *Australian Cultural History* no. 5, 1986, entitled 'Royal Progress: The Queen and her Australian subjects', Peter Spearritt wrote that the royal tour of 1954 was 'the most elaborate and most publicised sequence of events Australia has ever seen' (p. 88). The detail of a two-hour visit to Port Lincoln on one half day of 56 days overall supports that. Moreover, at the local level the visit was successfully turned into a popular festival or carnival. There is not the space here to talk about surrounding events at Port Lincoln – the royal cars were on display the day before, the foreshore was illuminated for the occasion making the whole area 'a fairy land of colour', there was a street procession of 36 floats on the morning of the visit, and afterwards community singing and square dancing to the town band outside the hall, a free dance inside, and a gala loyalty ball – nor is there room to elaborate on the extent of community participation. But the mayor was undoubtedly right to say in his thanks to the community that there was scarcely a person in Port Lincoln who was not represented by one of the many organisations involved in the preparations. The result was, he said, 'a masterpiece of cooperation'. The local paper concluded that the people of Port Lincoln probably had a better opportunity to see the Queen close up and in comfort than any in Australia and gave a headline to the fact that 'nobody fainted at Port Lincoln'.[9]

There were two aspects of the way in which the Queen's visit to Port Lincoln was marked out that would cause embarrassment or bemusement nowadays. Today a float representing the antics of

An illuminated address prepared by Mr H.A. Payze, Frankston Victoria.

ELIZABETH II

We have the honour to be

The royal car, a Humber, with the military lining the streets.
[J.H. Randall, *Port Lincoln Times* 25/3/1954]

The floral fan on Port Lincoln Oval, looking east from near the Royal Dais. [J.H. Randall, *Port Lincoln Times* 25/3/1954]

Floral fan dancers. [Nick Price]

'blackfellas' would not be condoned. Secondly, while it is easy enough to enter into the exuberance of it all, the underlying emotion is now quite remote. How, for instance, would younger Australians now react to the mayor's message on the eve of the visit encouraging people to show the royals 'that we love to have them with us, and are really pleased to see them'? With indifference, I would guess, though 'loyalty' is right back on the political agenda, and it is hard to predict how a new generation might respond to future royal visits. I have seen no evidence that anyone on Eyre Peninsula made negative remarks in 1954.[10]

It is impressive that this regional community showed itself capable of organising such a successful popular festival in the 1950s. Perhaps the fact that Eyre Peninsula is the most clearly defined region in South Australia, maybe even Australia, had something to do with it, also regional pride in the results of comparatively recent closer European settlement. However, if other regional visits were researched, it is likely that we would find that they all put their best foot forward in 1954. There is certainly no shortage of sources for such a project. The press coverage of the royal tour was phenomenal, and there were many spin-offs, usually lavish pictorials, such as *The Royal Tour of Australia and New Zealand in Pictures*, a publication of the *Herald and Sun News-Pictorial*, Melbourne, which includes a wonderful photo of the young Margaret Moles curtseying to the Queen at Mount Gambier. If reporters tended to run out of adjectives as the tour progressed, the photographers never missed an angle. (This was two years before the introduction of television.)

Some wider considerations

There are other wider considerations of the royal visit to do with regions. One way of thinking about this country is to see it as a mosaic of regions. However, in the course of research for an entry on Eyre Peninsula for that valuable work *The Wakefield Companion to South Australian History*, I found that ways of defining a region have changed over time, and especially the boundaries. It became clear that what the organisers of the 1954 royal tour seem to have understood about regions was a little different from today. In particular it was (rightly) thought important to include as many country centres in the royal itinerary as possible, and there were many side trips from the state capitals – but not to central or northern Australia, except for the Queensland coastal cities.[11]

Tempting as it is to go through the whole tour itinerary, this must be resisted, if only for reasons of space. But the side trips provide evidence of a mosaic of regions in the 1950s. In NSW, there were trips north to Newcastle and beyond, to Lismore and Casino; west to Dubbo (where one of my favourite images of regional pride was captured: a line up at the show of stud merinos, their backsides facing the Queen); south to Wollongong and to Bathurst; and lastly, south-east to Wagga Wagga, from which city the royals flew to Canberra for much pomp and circumstance. Even in the then sparsely inhabited Canberra, there was an impressive children's display.

After Sydney again, the royal entourage flew to Tasmania, where the Queen especially liked the climate – no wonder, it had been so hot in Sydney some 2000 people fainted in the streets on day one – and the towns along the north coast of the island state got special attention, and then back to Melbourne. The first Victorian side trip was, interestingly, to Mount Gambier in South Australia and Hamilton. There were two other trips from Melbourne – to Gippsland as far as Yallourn, and north to Echuca, with a swing back through Ballarat and Geelong. Then it was on to Brisbane, to take in Bundaberg, Toowoomba, and a circle with the *Gothic* north to sugar towns, as mentioned earlier.

By this time, it was South Australia's turn. The Queen and Prince Philip were in South Australia for a week, from 18–25 March. During that time they visited not only Eyre Peninsula, but also the weapons establishment at Woomera and the Riverland. If Mount Gambier had been counted as part of Victoria's Western District, Broken Hill and Mildura now came within the South Australian orbit. That done, it was then nearly all over, with the time in Western Australia restricted due to the polio outbreak. There the Queen went south to Albany, and only west as far as York (they called at Kalgoorie en route). The royal yacht *Gothic* sailed from Fremantle for London via Suez on 1 April 1954.

Everywhere it was the same, with pomp and circumstance, the wreaths, the children's displays, and important local industries, such as the sheep at Dubbo and the steelworks at Whyalla, to be inspected. By the time the Queen got back to London after her six-month tour around the world she had travelled an estimated 80,000 kilometres, attended 135 receptions, opened 6 parliaments, laid 7 wreaths, and watched 27 children's displays, to mention only her main duties. Obviously it was a young person's schedule, and if nothing else the monarch's stamina must be admired. Overall, the planning of the 1954 royal tour suggests it was a tour of now secure white settlements of the British Empire – that float of 'blackfellas' at Port Lincoln, a region of very recent closer settlement, springs to mind – at their most exuberant and assured.

Novelists and historians too were confident of the future of regions and regionalism in the 1950s. As the study of Australian history gradually established itself in the 1950s and 1960s, some fine regional studies appeared. Outstanding examples would be Margaret Kiddle's *Men of Yesterday* (1961) on the Western District of Victoria, Geoffrey Bolton's *A Thousand Miles Away* (1963) on Far North Queensland and D.B. Waterson, *Squatter, Storekeeper and Selector: A history of the Darling Downs 1859–93* (1968), also Robin Walker's *Old New England* (1966) and Gordon Buxton on *The Riverina, 1861–1891* (1967). This we now realise was a golden age of regional history, when it seemed the national story was becoming clear and it was a matter of filling in the gaps and finding fresh insights, acknowledging complexity and appreciating variety.

But that, we now see, was the old regionalism. As Maurice French has explained in the *Oxford Companion to Australian History*, things then began to look a bit bleak, though new approaches have been sought in different relationships or larger groupings. That worked well for John Hirst in *Adelaide and the Country* (1973). Another way to go is to see Australia itself as a region, and comparative studies seemed promising, for example with Argentina. The most innovative work to appear was W.K. Hancock's *Discovering Monaro,* published in 1972, which brought the environment in, showing among other things that it was only due to the Snowy Mountains project engineers' fear of water pollution that great tracts of the Australian Alps were spared the axe and the bulldozer.

A new regionalism?

Is a new regionalism in sight? If so maybe there will be a spot in it for Eyre Peninsula. After all, there has been a boom in local histories and family histories there, as elsewhere, since the 1960s. Local histories often do their job well, they are increasingly well produced and, although their purchase may not be wide, that is not the point. Two family histories which have come my way recently are *The Old Hands*, volume 1 of the Buddong books, a three-volume project documenting the families of the maternal forebears of writer Miles Franklin, originating in southern NSW and now a vast tribe scattered throughout eastern Australia, and the *Laube Family: 150 years in Australia 1854–2004*, which lays out this regional South Australian family's German background for the first time. It is notable also that an enormous amount of local history has come from the various state centenaries in the 1980s. South Australia seems to have been quite good at it, due to a combination of local energy, professional oversight and the care taken with production values.[12]

Local and family histories are adding new building bricks, even new layers, to our understanding and appreciation of regional history all the time. They stand for continuity – the ongoings, as it were. What of discontinuities? The major one of course has been the recognition of Aboriginal history, which seems to work best in regional frameworks. Mark McKenna's *Looking for Blackfellas' Point: An Australian history of place* (2002) is a good example. This beautifully produced book was inspired by the author's purchase of about four hectares, some 25 kilometres inland from Eden on the far south coast of NSW. From there he sees 'Blackfellas' Point'. Why is it called that? The question leads him into a little-studied region that tells us things we didn't know before and gets away from legalistic approaches to the historical realities. If McKenna does not quite write inclusive history he comes close. His idea of 'looking for' is a good one.

At this point I think again of Peggy Brock's *Outback Ghettoes* (1993), which examines the experience of Aboriginal people on the Lutheran missions on Eyre Peninsula. Like all good history, this book came to me with a shock of recognition. The story in *Outback Ghettoes* tells of things we didn't know before – perhaps we should have – and adds a new and, alas, a tragic dimension to the region's history. On a grander scale, the history of the Kimberley in Western Australia is being transformed by research into the Aboriginal experience, much of it distressing, none of it yet settled or fully integrated into the national story. This history may be hard for some to take in, but that is because it adds new data and a challenging dimension to taken-for-granted narratives. In time, along with environmental and the other histories, Indigenous history will most likely lead to a new regional history in this country. Personally, I don't expect to live long enough to see it, but it will come, not for any political reason but because it will be better history, meaning more accurate and more inclusive history. Maybe I should add my firm belief that any history in which people cannot recognise themselves – whether proudly or ruefully, in surprise or dismay – is not good history.

There is another dimension to regional history, which needs to be restored. It is the urban dimension. Working on the biography of Miles Franklin, I became aware that as a writer Miles owed as much to 1890s Goulburn as to Brindabella and the bush. Like many other provincial cities, Goulburn had all the skills and facilities needed to develop a literary talent. It was not hard to find what these skills and facilities were: the *Goulburn Evening Penny Post*, the Mechanics' Institute library, the Academy of Music, the two cathedrals, and not forgetting the annual show as a place to discover a wider world and to display schoolgirl talents. However, the only history of this historically significant regional city to date was published in 1941. It tells me a lot, but Goulburn deserves an update, possibly along the lines of a recent regional city history, *Colonial Armidale* (1999) by the late John Ferry, or Weston Bate on Ballarat, *Lucky City* (1978), a classic work. Perhaps it is the comparative neglect of the urban dimension in regional life that explains an apparent loss of interest and dynamism in rural life. Cities have always been great generators of health and wealth and, if the NSW experience is any guide, the larger of them have become more, not less, important over time, though not as important as seemed possible in the late 19th century, when optimism and British capital built little 'Victorian' cities all over rural and regional Australia.[13]

Mention should also be made of culture, by which I mean not only literature, art and music – of which there was and still is more than you might think outside the capital cities – but also sport. When I first turned my mind back to Eyre Peninsula in 1998, I paid no attention to sport as a source of social life and values, a mistake I must not make again. Sport, as much as geography, may define a community and a region. Indeed, I have heard it said that Australian Rules football is a religion on Eyre Peninsula. I would also be keen to see the churches more firmly treated as a source of social cohesion, certainly until very recently, perhaps still. The church of St Michael and All Angels, a tiny and too often vandalised ruin still to be seen right beside the Federal Highway between Canberra and Goulburn, springs irresistibly to mind. Here, aged 10, Miles Franklin first attended a public school. With teachers and clergy came the whole range of rural bourgeoisie who helped her so much (except for a thankfully short-lived singing teacher who she believed ruined her voice).[14]

Much has changed in the regions over the past 50 years, especially for the regions as regions. Take Goulburn again. Its handsome late Victorian buildings have now been restored along the main street, no longer a highway for interstate traffic, with few, if any, grotesque modern buildings to overshadow them. This is all to the good. But the wool sales are gone, and the old squatter families, some having been there for 200 years, are selling up. Without the jail, the asylum and the police academy – that is, without state institutions – it is doubtful if the once vibrant rural economy would be sufficient to sustain its 22,000-odd population. Fewer trains pass through, although this is the main Sydney–Melbourne line, and the old railway station is now a tourist information centre. Ironically, just as Goulburn is recovering its historical identity, it is becoming a residential outlier for Canberra, and the surrounding small towns offer weekenders for Sydney-siders.

Likewise, the world has changed for Eyre Peninsula as a region. It was a shock to me not so long ago to find how far the east–west highway has transformed the balance between north and south, and that Eyre Peninsula is now a popular tourist destination. When I first went to the eastern states in the 1960s, people seemed to find it amusing that I was born at Tumby Bay, though I never understood why. Now Tumby has a new suburb, its residents fly to Adelaide and back for the day, and writers boast about being born there.

Which brings me to one final, fundamental challenge to regional history. Some of the histories I've been citing are really about the colonial period. In modern times, the old songs of progress and development may not be so easy to sing and new darker sides show up, especially rural depopulation and health issues. When 'the man on the land' became 'Marlboro man', it was bad news. And what of the young? New South Wales has always had a substantial regional population, but even there the pull of the city seems unremitting. In South Australia, where it has always been a case of 'Adelaide and the country', the pull presumably has been similar. On the other hand, some will surely return, and some city dwellers are being drawn to the regions such as Eyre Peninsula by lifestyle factors and lower housing costs.

This chapter started from the royal visit to Port Lincoln and proceeded to 'think out loud' about ways of approaching regional history. Hopefully enough has been said to indicate that any new approach to regional history will have a lot more data to take in, that it will have to add some new dimensions, and that it will need to update its perspectives. Those of 50 years ago will no longer do. By now the Queen's visit to Port Lincoln seems like an exotic event, and more like the end of an era than the onset of a new one. Two generations have come into being since we danced for the Queen and so much has happened to us all since that it seems like another world, especially if we factor in the coming of television in the late 1950s. At the same time, it is a reminder that in regional history, people and place are the great constants.

CHAPTER 8

The Show

Yallunda Flat – the settlers – the Show – other perspectives

In 1997, at the urging of my sister Heather, and with an address to a conference of the Australian Historical Association (AHA) the following year in mind, I attended the Yallunda Flat Show for the first time since – could it be? – 1959. Heather said we should go again before we were too old to totter round the ring and, since the AHA conference convening committee had suggested as a subject, 'Your perspective on the virtues and problems of recent developments in the practice of history in Australia', it seemed like a promising idea. I had been wondering what my perspective would be for the address when an old school friend forwarded a copy of the 1997 *Show Book*. As soon as I saw the ad on the back cover, the die was cast, and indeed the topic took a life of its own, as all real research tasks do. Arguably, this was one I had been avoiding all my professional life. As a matter of fact, I wondered if it should not be done as a film. Alas, the person who could have made it, the great Graham Chase, who made *Cooee*, the Gilgandra March re-enactment, and *Modern Times*, on his birthplace Port Pirie, died about then.

What was it on the back cover of the *Show Book* that caught my eye? The astonishing answer is a photograph of a belly dancer,

Monique Hassan, who was advertised to give three twenty-minute performances between noon and 3 pm at the Music/Bandstand Rotunda. How extraordinary!

Yallunda Flat

The map of the Peninsula at the front of this book shows Yallunda Flat approximately halfway along the east–west road connecting Tumby Bay and Cummins, at which point there is also an intersection with a north–south road from Ungarra and beyond to Port Lincoln. The place name, which for me at least has a certain charm, dates back to the first peoples, the Parnkallas of the Nawu grouping. According to *Gum Trees and Gullies*, compiled by the Yallunda Flat Book Committee for the Jubilee 150 celebrations, the Parnkalla's word *yalla* meant 'flame, gale, storm, quick'.

These days Yallunda Flat is not much more than a road junction with a corrugated iron community hall and a showground-cum-sporting facility nearby, though for 50 years or more there was a shop (and post office), a church (1914–1963, Methodist), a school (one-teacher), and a war memorial pine plantation, all dating from the early 20th century. However, many Australians will have caught a glimpse of the locality, as the footrace in the film *Gallipoli* was run on the showground.

In early October 1997 I met my sister and a friend of hers at Whyalla airport. After a 'cuppa' in the red city, we drove up to Iron Knob (what is left of it) then west along the Eyre Highway through Kimba as far as Pygery, where we turned southwards to Port Lincoln. This way we saw most of what Peter Read, in his innovative but dispiritingly titled *Returning to Nothing* (1996), calls our 'lost places'. On the Monday, we were back at Yallunda Flat and the Show.

The Yallunda Flat Showgrounds in flood, 2014.
[Jim and Mandy Cabot]

It was a damp day and not quite the Show we remembered. However, Yallunda Flat was much the same picturesque place as in our youth, where several creeks converge and flash floods sometimes occur and affect the Show. Yallunda Flat is still a quiet place, too. The Tumby/Cummins through-traffic, along what is now known as Bratten Way, is probably its busiest feature. Nonetheless, like many small settlements in Australia, there has always been a strong sense of community and, at least in my day, numerous community events throughout the year. Of these events, the Show was, and remains, pre-eminent.

The settlers

Our grandmothers first saw this country less than a century earlier. In so far as can now be discerned, the reactions of those first-generation girls were not so very different from ours. An account written by Grandmother Roe reads as follows (incidentally, this is transcribed from my first ever research project, 'A Geographic Field Survey of the Hundreds of Hutchinson and Koppio, Eyre Peninsula, South Australia,' undertaken in fulfilment of the requirements of Leaving Certificate Geography):

> In the springtime of 1903 we Gilbert and Anna Roe set out to see the beauties of a new part . . . [We] came by Wallaroo by steamer to Port Lincoln, stayed at the hotel there. Mr Dan Green was the proprietor then, and from him we hired ponies and buggy. We started off; the drive was wonderful. Our first port of call was Mrs Tucknotts for water to make a pot of tea. The grass was beginning to dry off, and it was not safe to boil the billy. The kindness lavished on travellers made it well worth bumping over stumps, stones and gutters. . . . Then we journeyed on, past Yallunda Flat (Bhola Sha) to 'Kapinka' where we stayed the night. The next morning we started out with the 'North Block' and 'Marble Range' as our guiding stars. First we decided to cut through scrub and straight down the side of the Range (without mishap). After a few miles we came across a little plain & mud hut on it. There we got boiling water for tea, had our lunch and continued along the peg-line. Over low mallee the ponies could jump & drag the buggy on top of bushes. In some cases bushes had to be held back while I drove. Reached block one at last and took a look around from this high position . . . We were delighted with the view from every side. . . . The promised land thrilled us.[1]

Here you can catch the cadences of the King James Version of the Bible. The Willamunka Roes were Bible Christians, like that fiery suffragist Serena Thorne Lake in Helen Jones's *In Her Own Name: Women in South Australian History* (1986). The next generation became Methodists with the union of Wesleyan groups in 1900. Probably something was lost. By 1907, Gilbert and Anna Roe were settled with their family on a substantial and well-situated farm of over 800 hectares (presumably rented at first and then under purchase in accordance with closer settlement legislation) at what they called 'Marble View', where they soon had an organ and people gathered to sing from Sankey's hymnal. 'Marble View' was near to, but not strictly speaking of, Yallunda Flat, and adjacent to the Hundreds of Koppio and Stokes where Yallunda Flat is situated. This explains why Gilbert Roe appears in a 1907 photograph of the Yallunda Flat Sports Committee, a precursor of the Central Eyre Peninsula Agricultural and Horticultural (A and H) Society, renamed from the 1940s the Yallunda Flat Agricultural and Horticultural Society.

There is a small literature and some data on the peopling of the inner districts of Lower Eyre Peninsula. It shows that the peopling came late and at speed between 1901 and 1921. In 1901 the recorded population of the Hundred of Koppio, where most of Yallunda Flat is located, amounted to a mere 40 persons. (We cannot be sure how many Parnkallas that excluded, but it could not have been many, as it seems the last of the clan died about this time.) By 1921 census collectors' books indicate there were 430 persons, a tenfold increase. That proved to be an all-time high. Numbers had almost halved by 1933, when the figure stood at 232. The figure for Koppio for the year 1966 was 260. Numbers are unlikely to have increased since then.[2]

Fortunately for the historian, the census figures are sex-specific. No wonder women were valued in the country: at first there were very few, due to pastoral policy. As the newcomers found, and John Hirst noticed in *Adelaide and the Country* (1973), bachelors were preferred on the runs, and closer settlement did not at first mean more women. In 1901, of the 40 persons enumerated on census night in the Hundred of Koppio, there were 27 males and 13 females. By 1921, it was worse: 311 males to 119 females. But a more balanced demography developed thereafter, so that while it appears the district has always had more males than females, things evened out. By 1947 there were 113 males and 107 females recorded.

Few though they were at first, the women tended to live longer than the males, as did both my grandmothers. Alas, I did not hear enough of their stories. But, thanks largely to the Jubilee 150 celebrations in 1986, many other stories have been collected, and they make interesting reading today, when we are well attuned to such texts. I have room for only two such stories, of the first 'overlander', Mrs Olston (her other names unknown), and Henrietta Fuss, later Durdin. They were among the very earliest arrivals at Yallunda Flat. The Olston family of eight left Peterborough in the state's north-east in 1902 with six strong horses and a pony, arriving at their Koppio allotment via Port Augusta some six weeks later. Mrs Olston drove the pony cart all the way and made their daily bread. Five months later, she gave birth to 'the first white boy in the settlement' and they called him John Koppio. She survived all that, but not the death of her eldest son in the Great War a decade later – never a strong woman, they said. Like the Olstons, Henrietta Fuss' family also came from the 'dry dusty north', near Orroroo, in 1903. The Fusses travelled by boat from Port

Pirie to Tumby Bay, but then they had to walk over the hills to their block. When they arrived it was 'just all scrub'. But, Henrietta recalled, the next morning they were woken by a strange sound, and when they saw that it was a kookaburra they felt it was 'welcoming us to our new home' (actually the reverse would more likely be the case since, if I understand it correctly, kookaburras laugh to define their territory). 'We thought the kookaburra was wonderful', the memory continues, 'and in the fresh morning, the sunlight falling on the trees and the bush, everything so strange and beautiful, it seemed more cheerful' (both stories from *Gum Trees and Gullies*, 1986).

The story of Anne Angela Liddy (1901–1986), a trained nurse whose memories were recorded in 1985, is held in the Mortlock Library, Adelaide. She was born at Dawson in the state's Upper North into an Irish Catholic family 'with a genius for going to dry places where they don't make any money'. The Liddys arrived about 1904 and Anne attended Yallunda Flat School until 1914, when the family went bankrupt. Anne Liddy then entered domestic service, and left the district in the mid-1920s. Not all those who took part in the second phase of settlement of Eyre Peninsula flourished there.

According to South Australian geographer the late Les Heathcote, Koppio is one of the few hundreds where boundaries have remained unchanged over time. This is a reminder of the prior pastoral age, which dates from a special survey in 1839, and of people already there when the folk movement of small farmers from the north-east of the state began in the late 19th century. The reality was that, although much of the country was 'just scrub', the newcomers were not starting completely from scratch, nor was all the land in the district unclaimed. It seems that, when the pastoral leases expired in 1867, the land was surveyed, a hundred was proclaimed, and sections were put up for auction. As happened during comparable transitions elsewhere in Australia, a few farms resulted, but also some large freehold pastoral estates. Even after most of the old Koppio Station was resumed and subdivided in 1901 in accordance with 1890s closer settlement legislation – thus creating the basis for farming at Yallunda Flat – there were still some big estates in the district. Kapinka, where Gilbert and Anna Roe stayed in 1903, was one of them. The ownership of Kapinka changed in 1904, but the estate remained substantial until 1959, when sections were resumed for soldier settlement. While the ubiquitous William Ranson Mortlock lost some land at Koppio in 1868 to the Borthwick family and others, the family held Yalluna Station for almost as long (it was resumed for soldier settlement in 1949). By the late 19th century some of the early landholders had left but others, by choice and/or necessity, stayed on to make the most of changing circumstances. According to the *Australian Dictionary of Biography*, J.H. Browne, owner of Koppio Station, lived in Bath, UK, from 1870, but Tom Borthwick was born at Pillaworta in 1893 and spent his entire life there.

Pillaworta, Koppio, Yallunda, Kapinka – even now these 19th century names have a ring to them, and some purchase. Although the once considerable stations such as at Koppio are no more, the ethos did not entirely seep away. Received historical wisdom has it that in South Australia small farmers had 'a better chance' against the pastoralists, due to Wakefieldian influences – the requirement of survey before settlement, for example – and to environmental factors, such as a drier climate more suited to the growing of wheat and other crops. But the late 19th century auctions still favoured the big men, and a balanced view seems to be that both farmers and resident pastoralists did slightly better under the more closely regulated conditions obtained in South Australia from the 1880s.

So far I have merely hinted at the characteristics and circumstances that seem to have ensured the successful settlement by small farmers on the interior lands of Lower Eyre Peninsula, and – I will come to it shortly – the success of the Show. But for a moment we must persist with 'the frontier', another topical subject. In *Bush and Backwoods*, a comparative essay on the frontier in Australia and America published way back in 1959, British historian H.C. Allen noted that the wheat-producing areas of South Australia were comparable to those of the American frontier:

> This was the first region of Australia in which relatively small farmers were able to succeed in the way that they were able to do in the whole of the Northeast and Middle West of the United States. (p. 50)

From the historiography, we might expect some distinctive developments in the regions under consideration. And maybe there were, though, as Geoffrey Bolton has stressed in a more general context, some subtlety is required to detect them. Twenty years on, a second generation of small farmers would test the farming frontier on Eyre Peninsula to its limits. That was up Pygery way in the interwar years, when the rail and a pipeline enabled a third phase of white settlement on Eyre Peninsula to proceed, and the further occupation of interior lands. That occupation is another, rather better-known, story, involving, as it does, Goyder's line and soldier settlement up north, and further out still, around Koonibba Mission, the final, tragic, exclusion of Aboriginal Australians from farming. Of particular relevance here is the attention paid to cultural factors in recent research. Thus Canadian historical geographer David Wood, presenting a sliver of his comparative researches in the *Journal of Historical Geography* (23, 4, 1997) entitled 'Limits Reaffirmed: New wheat frontiers in Australia, 1916–1939', writes that 'the farming people who were going into new areas to grow crops had a good idea of what was needed to sustain their settlement', and that 'within five years of the arrival of the first wheat farmers [in the Wudinna area], there is evidence of a social structure taking shape' (p. 463). From a historical if not an economic point of view, this seems to be an advance on past formulations, for example:

> The ideal of a self-supporting yeomanry was gone and in its place there had emerged the reality of a foot-loose population engaged in a business-like approach to agriculture, specialising in wheat growing for a world-wide competitive market.[3]

It's not the word 'business-like' that jars, it's 'foot-loose'. If you look up the community history *Gum Trees and Gullies*, from which I draw a good deal, the final section is headed 'Families'. A few of them have been there for well over a century – the family of international tennis player John Fitzgerald for example – and a number date from the turn-of-century subdivision of Koppio Station. There are pictures of (I think) one of Henrietta Fuss's sons, and many Cabot families, whose progenitors came from or via San Francisco and Johannesburg in 1904. Michael and Caryll Cabot are today's Show stalwarts. The following sentence on the now-departed Roe family also appears in *Gum Trees and Gullies*: 'In later years . . . the family of four girls, Pauline, Jean, Heather and Jill, were to undertake career training which was to take them away from the district' (p. 149). Maybe we were the 'foot-loose' aspect.

Wood's notion of a social structure within five years readily relates to the community at Yallunda Flat. On the one hand, the old pastoral age melded with the new agricultural era. The newcomers were grateful for hot water, the shepherds' huts gave shelter along the way, and stores were available from Bolah Shah, the Indian hawker referred to by Anna Roe, who was also a member of the early Sports Committee. On the other hand, the newcomers soon made their mark. It's difficult now to imagine hand-sown crops, but spirits must have been high, with picnics and sports days dating almost from arrival. At a masquerade ball held at Yallunda Flat in 1904 – one wonders where, as the provisional school did not open until the following January, so perhaps in a barn or woolshed – the new-comers danced the Lancers, Polka, Mazurka, Alberts, Schottische and the Croat Polka, maybe to fiddle and drum, and there were costume prizes and a lucky dip. There were at least 18 children ready for schooling the following year (a handwritten list recalling the first pupils survives in my school project), and 20 in 1908. In the years before World War I, it is written, 'Yallunda Flat went ahead'. Possibly even the roads improved somewhat as the hundreds were brought under district council governance in 1906, and by then there were 'preaching places' as well as sports clubs.[4]

The show

The first Show was held at Yallunda Flat on Thursday 12 November 1908. As reported the following week in the *Port Lincoln, Tumby, and West Coast Recorder* (November 18, 1908) it was 'a splendid success', with between seven and eight hundred people attending. Doubts about accessibility and the proliferation of country shows were dispelled, and the primary objects of a show – that is the betterment of stock, produce, and rural industries – were deemed upheld. The picturesque venue was greatly praised, also the quality of the exhibits, especially the horses, where Gilbert Roe unexpectedly turns up as a judge. There were nine or so sections for exhibits, these being horses, sheep, poultry, green fodder and produce, home produce, vegetables, flowers, miscellaneous (fancy work) and schoolwork (it is not clear about dogs and pigs), and a hundred pounds worth of prizes had been donated. A reported 700 entries indicate a ready response, as do the lists of winning classes published in the *Recorder*, for example, for poultry there were 13 prize-winning classes, mainly Leghorn, Wyandotte, and Orpington but also Plymouth Rock and Indian Game, plus ducks and turkeys. Miss A. Palm carried off 12 of the indoor prizes: three in home produce (two 2 lb loaves of bread, yeast buns, scones), two for vegetables (a peck of green peas, three bunches of onions), six for flowers including wildflower, plus one for fancy work. There was a wood-chopping contest at the first Show (in *The Grand Parade*, a history of the Royal Agricultural Society of New South Wales, Brian Fletcher notes that wood-chopping was introduced to the Sydney Show in 1899, so Yallunda Flat was not far behind), a live sheep's weight guessing competition, and sideshows. Aged 90, Robert Stanley Campbell gave a child's point of view of the day:

> It was a great day for us all when the first Show was held at Yallunda Flat. There was a public booth [a bar tent], a hurdy-gurdy driven by two men, one an Indian chap who was a bit under the weather. 'Come on Shawldren,' he said, 'have a free ride for threepence.'[5]

In the evening, with the Show itself over, there was a concert and dance in the newly opened community hall, the one that's still there, lasting into 'the small hours'. The prize-winning Miss Palm was one of the concert performers.

A visiting school inspector is reported as saying he had 'no idea we had advanced so far as to provide an up-to-date show like Yallunda Flat'. As indeed it was. The *Recorder* reveals that the Show Committee intended to make something special of it, a popular picnic event like the Onkaparinga Race Meeting, meaning Oakbank, Adelaide's version of the Bong Bong races, which began in the 1870s.

During the Show's first decade, things went extremely well, even the weather, and, despite the 1914–1918 war, attendances increased, passing the 1000 mark in 1912. People came from all the surrounding districts, and from further afield, increasingly in cars. And the Show Committee ensured that there was more to see and do. There were 'entirely satisfactory' entries across an extended range of classes by 1912, both outdoor and indoors, with good work and jumping horses, superior wool on the sheep, excellent green oats, wonderful cabbages and so on outdoors (pigs, dogs and cattle seem not so strong, however), and indoors already a feature. The accomplished Miss Palm again carried off many prizes. War brought uncertainty, but the Show went on. In 1917 there was a prize for woollen comforters, and the concert closed with 'God Save the King', 'The Soldier's Hymn' and the 'Song of Australia'. Gate takings in 1917 were reported as 'the highest ever recorded'.

In 1997 when Heather and I visited, the Yallunda Flat A and H Society was in its 90th year (though only its 85th Show, due to a pause in World War II, when there were sports days instead). It is not now quite so assured, and there is no doubt some underlying anxiety. The question is, of course, can it survive? Not many institutions last over a century in Australia, and the chances of a small community being able to sustain from its own resources an ever-more demanding commitment may seem slim, but in 2013 it successfully celebrated the 100th Show, and it is a case of 'so far so good'.

The Show Heather and I visited was still doing well. It was a bit muddy under foot, but bright green because of the rain. We managed the walk around the ring with ease: anticlockwise, down past the hall and the pavilion; around to watch the belly dancer at the rotunda (she seemed very young and brave on the day); on through the horse floats to pause among a string of stalls on the southern slope to eat and chat; then on to see the animals and farm produce, before inspecting the indoor exhibits in the hall and the sheep-shearing competition in the afternoon. As those present wandered about in jeans and other casual clothes, I was reminded of how once people had dressed up for the occasion. For me and my sisters, the Show had meant 'the one dress of the year' – by which I do not mean we wore trousers at other times, but that we girls got new dresses for that day. They would be our 'best dresses' until the next Show.

Inspecting the indoor exhibits was always an enjoyable experience, due especially to the cakes section, where fruitcakes, sponge cakes and crème puffs were among the main attractions. In Liz Harfull's *The Blue Ribbon Cake Book*, subtitled *Recipes, stories and tips from prizewinning country show cooks*, published in 2008, the winner at Yallunda Flat at that time was Kimba-born Dot Brougham, who provided a recipe for jubilee cake, a traditional staple that is gradually disappearing from the cookery schedules (p. 162). Harfull's splendidly produced book encompasses some 50 country shows across South Australia, including seven from Eyre Peninsula, at Yallunda Flat, Cleve, Cummins, Kimba, Port Lincoln, Ungarra, and Whyalla, established as recently as 1971. I

Yallunda Flat Showground, 2003, with (top left) the dog jumping competition, and (above right) horse-and-wagon rides.

went to most of them, though I could never have produced anything worth entering in the cakes sections.

A number of Australians seem to be reporting anxiously on their rural and country town childhoods these days. Bob Ellis has been worrying about his aged mother at Murwillumbah and Michael Pusey reports that it's 'meltdown' in his bit of Tasmania. But one of my ex-colleagues, now alas deceased, decided to retire to Cootamundra. So before lapsing into gloom as yet another rural community seems to be weakened by forces beyond its control, forces that in this case may briefly be summarised as consumerist, there is something more cheering to be said on the basis of historical evidence – several things in fact.

First, regarding attendance. Figures over time point to the rise and then a relative, but not catastrophic, decline in the popularity of Yallunda Flat's 'one day of the year'. In 1947 attendance at the Show had reached nearly 3000, and in 1957 it was double that at 6000, as it was again in 1977. But then it started to fall. Five years later, in 1982, the reported attendance was 3500, and by 1997 there were probably about 2000 present. However, the Show was still doing better than in the 1920s, and against stronger odds, and in 2013 some 5000 people would turn out for its centenary.

Second, natural advantage runs like a mantra through the press reports, from 1908 to now. A random quote, from the 1960s, sums that aspect up: 'the picturesque grounds set in a natural amphitheatre beneath shady gum trees make the show a favourite picnic ground'. In 1947 it was said 'all roads lead to Yallunda Flat'. Now they are bitumen roads, and it is a lot easier to get there. Moreover the area surrounding the hall seems to be well maintained and the hall is still in use for other events.

Third, the Show has always been a barometer of change in the rural culture, as the ups and down of pig exhibits may suggest – a co-researcher in 1997 remarked poetically that pigs are the will-o'-the-wisp of the Yallunda Flat Show. (I've since been told that pigs have been deleted due to the risk of diseases and the ever-increasing technicalities of animal husbandry.) Our researches into the changing 'shape' of the Show indicate that horses, sheep and chooks have held their own – though the type of horses has changed fundamentally, from work to leisure classes, and the perseverance of chooks is an interesting question – but cattle have not been on the lists for years (deleted for the same reason as pigs). The indoor displays have changed the most, and evidently contracted a lot, even though there are many more classes, such as for cookery: in 1917 there were 16 classes, in 1997, 34. The 'best-dressed fowl' disappeared from the *Show Book* in 1967. However, the varieties of handicrafts seem to go on forever, and new things like photography are popular.

They say country shows are dying out in some places. It is also said that historians only take an interest when things are on the way out. But Australian Rules football seems to have survived the attentions of historians in the 1970s, and I have often found that my interest encourages people, in their religious commitments for example. My final comment on the evidence would be that the Yallunda Flat Show people must have been doing some things right for the Show to last so long. They seem to have been alert to cultural change from the outset, as in the early aspiration to become a west coast Oakbank – which given the strength of the horses section, may yet still come to pass, though it would surely be a pity. Some of the adaptations may seem a bit bizarre, and of late maybe even a bit frenzied. But there's nothing bizarre about concluding with 'a splendid programme of pictures' in 1922. In 1927 the equestrian events began with three car races – and one of the cars backed into another afterwards, to the great amusement of all. In 1932, there was the introduction of amplified music from the centre of the ring. I referred earlier to the sheep-shearing competition, instituted in 1951. And so on, to the 1980s and 1990s, when we come upon the introduction of women's classes in the sheaf tossing, and an amazingly incorrect Showgirl competition. Then in 1997 it was the belly dancer.

On longevity, it seems obvious that this is not a question Australian historians have thought much about. Maybe I am missing something, but I have already cited the relevant works to appear in research journals such as *Australian Historical Studies* in the year prior to that first trip back to the Show. In any event, what has enabled it to last so long must surely be a prior question to whether it can survive. The fact is that over time a tiny rural town of no particular importance has done one thing well. How so? The explanation lies, I think, not only in natural advantage, and beautiful places, but also a stable and confident community. For instance, we found that early prize-winners often grew up to give prizes themselves, and many went on exhibiting for years, such as good old Mrs Lovegrove, who in 1982 won the prize in a new handicrafts class, over-70s knitting. Responsiveness has been important too. A Show should not only be useful, but fun. We found plenty of evidence of both aspects. And by now pride in longevity itself is a factor. Whether or not the Yallunda Flat Show is still there in future decades, its survival and ongoing strength is certainly something to celebrate.

Other perspectives

Kathleen Norris's book *Dakota: A spiritual geography* (1993) has been a best seller. In the 1970s Norris, a baby-boomer poet, and her husband returned from New York to live in her grandmother's house in Lemmon, an isolated border town in western South Dakota, on the far edge of the Great Plains. Lemmon (population 600) dates from 1908, when state legislation finally yielded to pressure and opened the last piece of Indian Territory to homesteaders, and agronomists predicted that rain would follow the plough, or at least the railway. This area is now 'the forgotten interior' and it was badly afflicted by the farm crisis of the 1980s. On return Norris found the Plains 'unforgiving' and denial everywhere. Over a year, in her book, she reflects on the prospects of renewal. Dakota is full of 'good telling stories', but she is clear about the realities of an inward-looking and in some respects self-defeating community. One section is entitled 'Can one tell the truth in a small community?' Her own effort as a teacher of creative writing is to unlock the stories, including those of native Americans. Unexpectedly she finds herself making a spiritual return, too – 'a person is forced inward by the sparseness' – and becomes a local preacher, almost by default. Most astonishing, she also becomes an oblate of several local Benedictine communities. Monasticism and the fourth-century world of the desert fathers is a constant reference point of *Dakota*. Norris knows that one person's frontier is usually another person's homeland, but comes to think that 'the one thing that distinguishes a frontier is the precarious nature of the human hold on it' (p. 127). These unlikely sources enable her to reconstruct some kind of 'spiritual geography', and to suggest that there may be important lessons to be learned from the distant wisdom of Dakota. As well, life in the slow lane, and the long view, lead her to hope, tentatively, that maybe she has been there long enough to say she belongs.

What, you say, is it back to Grandma and the pew? No, that's her story, and it's a very American story. What's ours? Like the land, still hanging, I'd say. My approach is post-modern in the sense that it can't come to a definite conclusion, but in my review of research journals I came upon an obituary for Russel Ward, and I thought the call for a more realistic view of the context and methodology of his shaping text *The Australian Legend* (1958) entirely justified. By now it is one book among many, and it has been the whipping boy for long enough, rarely read but attacked for much of what it was thought to say as well as for everything it was supposed to have left out. It was a different world in 1958, trapped as we were in Cold War rigidities. *The Legend* lifted cultural understandings clear of those constraints, and brought to the fore the role of the bush in shaping Australian consciousness.

More specifically, if we don't already know them, we should learn what Richard J. Evans identifies in *In Defence of History* (1997) as the positive lessons of post-modernism, regarding subjects, sources and style. This will assist us to re-visit and re-read the national story more effectively, taking in especially what Janet McCalman has called 'The originality of ordinary lives' (*Creating Australia*, 1995), and to focus more faithfully on 'the Australian way', as formulated in *Contesting the Australian Way* (1995), edited by Bettina Cass and Paul Smyth. It is a way we seem to have lost sight of, or are at best groping painfully towards. As Don Watson reminds us in his big and sometimes tantalising book entitled *The Bush* (2014), the issues addressed by Ward in the 1950s are ongoing, at once complex and inescapable.

Briefly, by way of conclusion, when I first embarked on this subject I attempted to put into practice what I felt should be preached. No doubt the very virtues and weaknesses I was asked then to look at are still all too evident. Land legislation is not a lot of fun either. But some things don't change that much, and the choices are not necessarily those presented by politicians, or, for that matter ,what historians have been focused on in recent times. By now Australian history is, or can be, of itself a major resource in the survival stakes. This is by no means an original conclusion, I know. The importance of grounded-ness over time was foreshadowed by the great nativist writers Joseph Furphy and Miles Franklin several generations ago but again that is another story, and I only mention it because it would be totally out of character not to.

CHAPTER 9

Survival: The Aboriginal experience

at first – a reality check – Elliston – the Stuart case – through a glass darkly

A comprehensive account of the Aboriginal experience of Eyre Peninsula has yet to be written. Maybe it can't be done, due to the vast time span to be encompassed, and until more Aboriginal people feel able to present their stories as Mercy Glastonbury has done in her fictonalised memoir, *Mazin Grace* (2012), the coverage of recent times must remain incomplete. However, new evidence is emerging, for example in native title hearings, and new understandings are in the making. Thus fresh light has recently been cast on this difficult and challenging subject by South Australian historians Robert Foster and Amanda Nettelbeck in their ground-breaking book *Out of the Silence* (2012), and much of interest and importance may be gleaned from the work of other researchers, and from the memoirs of early settlers. As well, older residents are now being encouraged to remember knowing Aboriginal people, and some are finding them hidden in their family histories. Perhaps, like me, they went to school with Aboriginal children in the early 1950s.[1]

At first

As has previously been noted, Aboriginal presence in the Eyre Peninsula region dates back maybe as far as 50,000 years, an estimate based on current understandings of the pre-history of three main groupings: the Nawu, the Banggarla and the Wirangu. The map from the *Encyclopedia of Aboriginal Australia* (1994) shows their respective locations when the Europeans first appeared, with Nawu territory in the south extending to about halfway up the west coast, the Banggarla lands on the east coast reaching from near Cowell to well into the

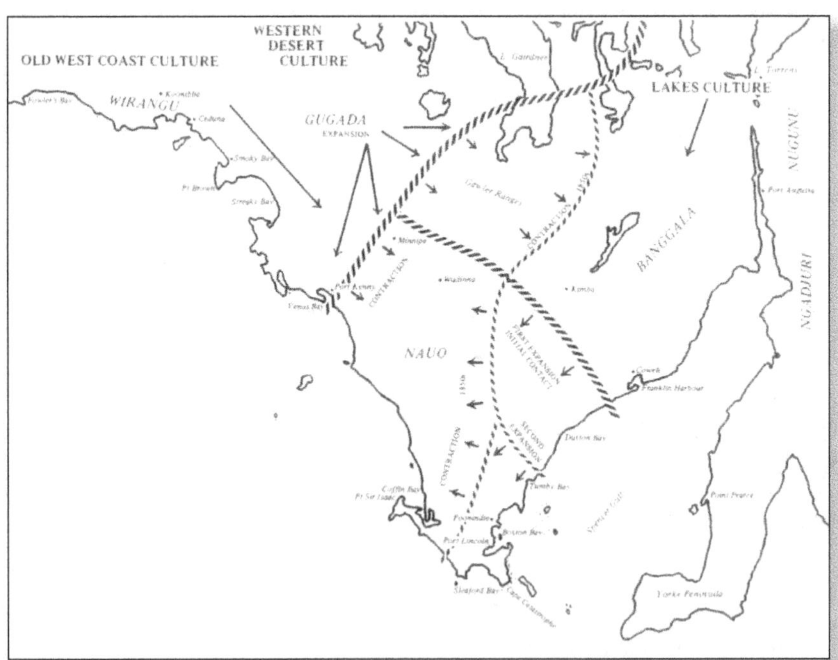

Expansion and contraction of Aboriginal groups on Eyre Peninsula during early European settlement.

[*Natural History of Eyre Peninsula*]

semi-arid north, and the Wirangu lands in the far west stretching from beyond Streaky Bay and Ceduna to the eastern edge of the Nullarbor Plain and a way into the interior.

How many Aboriginal people there were in the region before European colonisation in 1836 remains a matter of surmise. If, as has been estimated, the Aboriginal population for South Australia in 1788 was approximately 15,000, presumably there would not have been very many on Eyre Peninsula at that time, a few thousand maybe. To this may be added that, remote and cut off from the rest of Australia as the original occupants of the region may seem to have been, they had some contact with the wider world: ochre traders from Central Australia reached Port Augusta and further south in pre-contact times, and whalers and sealers from Kangaroo Island had established bases along the southern tip of the Peninsula and up the west coast by the early 19th century. Maybe some traditional owners even encountered the escaped convict said to have settled on an island in lower Spencer Gulf about then.[2]

Fascinating as these possibilities are, it remains the case that very little is known about the first peoples' lives on Eyre Peninsula in pre-colonial times. Explorer Matthew Flinders, who charted the coastline in 1802, well before colonisation, noted that 'Many struggling bark huts . . . were seen upon the shores of Port Lincoln, and the paths near or tents had been long and deeply trodden'. But he was reluctant to initiate contact with the local people, believing 'they would usually come down after having watched us for a few days'.[3]

Oral history may yet take us further into a world remote in every respect, but for now we must rely on what archaeologists and anthropologists have been able to tell us about the workings of family groups and larger bands and the daily life of hunter-gatherers – when the men hunted for protein and women gathered plant food – and, more broadly; about how these ways of life were underpinned by complex structures of belief known as 'the Dreaming'. These days we know much more about prior Aboriginal cultures than even a generation ago, for instance about inland pathways and fishing in coastal and riverbank communities, and for present purposes it probably suffices to say that this was a world slow to change, that a kind of sufficiency built up over a very long period of time pertained.[4]

It also remains the case that, even if more were known about the prior experience of the peoples and cultures of the region, it would be difficult to recapture in words the shock and upset caused by the arrival of European colonists on the tip of the Peninsula in 1839. As the now-deceased Aboriginal Anglican deacon of Roper River origins, Ken Hampton (1935–1987), wrote in an eloquent postscript to *Survival in Our Own Land*, a South Australian sesquicentenary publication told mainly by the Nungas themselves, it was a long, hard struggle thereafter, but 'we have survived'. Audrey Kinnear/Ngingali Cullen (1942–2012), the distinguished Aboriginal health worker from Kokatha/Pitjantjatjara country, inland from Denial Bay, has written in like vein: 'Life has not always been a bed of roses. It has been a long hard struggle for my own survival, and also to assist in paving the way for others'.[5]

Ngingali Cullen's story is a significant instance of the Aboriginal experience originating in Eyre Peninsula. Aged four, she was sent down to Koonibba and later to Concordia College, then a small but well-regarded Lutheran boarding school in Adelaide. Subsequently a health worker at Port Augusta, she rose to serve as first chair of the South Australian Aboriginal Health Commission, and in the 1990s with ATSIC in Canberra, where she became co-chair of the National Sorry Day Committee. It may not be easy to find others like her in the records right now, but oral history will surely uncover more significant 'survivors', even from such distant parts, and *Survival in Our Own Land* devotes many pages to the success of Aboriginal people in diverse fields in South Australia in recent times.[6]

A reality check

By the 1930s the estimated Aboriginal population of South Australia had fallen to fewer than 3000. However, a decade on, when recovery and assimilation were becoming the watch-words Australia-wide, an estimate based on the 1947 census made by anthropologists Ronald and Catherine Berndt in *From Black to White in South Australia* (1951) suggested that numbers had improved by then to over 4000. A more recent estimated minimum of all persons of Aboriginal descent in South Australia in 1947 published in the bicentennial volume *Australians: Historical statistics* (1987) is 5600, rising to 6300 in 1954.[7]

Even with an overall increase in the state's Aboriginal population by the 1950s, it is unlikely that there were as many as a thousand throughout Eyre Peninsula by then. If schoolgirls like me hardly noticed Aboriginal people at that time, it was partly because there were so few of them in our area (though not by then in the larger towns, where they gravitated in search of work). Nonetheless I, and no doubt others, can well recall 'the Betts kids'. If I remember correctly, there were four at Cummins Area School in my time. The two girls, Doris and her quieter sister, whose name I recall as May, sat unobtrusively at the back of the class. The boys were more conspicuous because they were good at Australian Rules football. I now know that some time earlier the Betts family left Koonibba and came south looking for work, and that Eddie Betts really was a champion footballer.[8]

At this point comes a reality check. Some 35 years later, on Tuesday 6 October 1987, Eddie (Edward Frederick) Betts died in Port Lincoln Police Station, aged 49. His travails and those of his family are fully recorded in an Aboriginal Deaths in Custody report of 1991. The report makes sad reading. By the 1960s Eddie was at the height of his success as a footballer, and married with a job on the Port Lincoln docks. But his health was giving out, and, when the docks were mechanised, Eddie became unemployed, living for the rest of his life on an invalid pension. It was probably inevitable that, like so many Aboriginal Australian men at that time, he took up the grog, and it was the grog that did for him in the end. The 1991 report written by well-respected Adelaide lawyer Elliott Johnston QC may suggest some criticism of those who had to deal with Betts *in extremis* is warranted, but it seems their impatience was understandable. Eddie was admitted to Port Lincoln Hospital at approximately 4 am and, according to the Johnston report, given suitable treatment but, against medical advice, discharged himself some six-and-a-half hours later, possibly suffering from withdrawal. It was a brief escape. He was readmitted to the hospital at 12.15 am and, when the attending doctor was unable to calm him, sent to the police station, where he died in a cell shortly before 2 pm. Neither the doctor nor the jailers were blamed for his death, which was attributed to heart disease. Members of his long-suffering family did their best to stick by him and have remained residents of the town.[9]

In some respects, Eddie was his people's experience writ large. However, as presently understood at least, his is a 20th century story, and hardly a representative one at that, given the small proportion of Aboriginal families who passed through the Koonibba Mission, itself a 20th century institution. Even so, it was a highly publicised case from the Peninsula as it came before the Aboriginal Deaths in Custody inquiry. During what was by all accounts an extended colonial experience, Aboriginal people often seem to be little more than a shadowy presence, and, if it were not for court records, few from the 19th century could now be named. Of those who can be named, almost all are men.

There is a good reason for this. These days it is generally agreed that Eyre Peninsula was South Australia's most violent frontier, and that something approximating war occurred around Port Lincoln in the early 1840s. At that time the Aboriginal population far outstripped that of the white colonisers and in 1842 they made numerous attacks on pastoral outstations, with near disastrous effects for the would-be settlers. Some prominent pastoralists were killed on the spot. Others left the area, most notably Charles Dutton, who left in July 1842, intending to drive his cattle overland to Adelaide. He disappeared without a trace somewhere beyond present-day Cleve, presumed to have been killed by remote Aboriginal people. So it was that, in the words of heritage consultants Susan Marsden and John Dallwitz, 'Of all places of European settlement in South Australia, Port Lincoln came closest to abandonment'. Having more recently reviewed the evidence of 'fearful and protracted conflict', Foster and Nettelbeck have concluded that what happened there came closer to European-style warfare than anything else that occurred at that time in South Australia.[10]

'Once were warriors'? If so, not many of them were captured and brought before the courts in 1842, and those who were, were seldom leaders of the attacks. Nor can those few who were captured be cast in an especially heroic light. However, their names do appear in the court records: for example Morldalta for his part in the killing of pastoralist John Brown and his hut keeper at Brown's station; Ngarbli, implicated in three deaths at Long Pond over the hill from Port Lincoln; Ngarka and Ngula, arrested after the attack by some 200 tribesmen on Charles Driver's inland hill station, 'Pillaworta'; and Merltalla and Nataltie, captured when assisting the Deputy Protector of Aborigines from 1840 to 1843, Clamor Schumann, in his search for the perpetrators of other recent murders. Yultalta, one of Schumann's guides, is also there in the records.[11]

Except for the killing of explorer John Charles Darke by 'the natives' in the interior in 1844, things seem to have calmed down somewhat after 1842. But hostilities flared up again as pastoralists made their way up the west coast in the later 1840s. There the Aboriginal population may have been spread thinly, but so were the pastoralists. Hence the pattern of the early 1840s was to be repeated in the later 1840s and the 1850s. By the 1860s, when the invaders had more staying power and better guns, the situation was again looking grim, though for a different reason. By then hunger had become a basic issue. As Aboriginal people were excluded from more land, they lost their traditional hunting grounds. By 1860 it had become necessary to set aside 14 small reserves – that is feeding stations – across the state. Four were on Eyre Peninsula, with more to come.[12]

In 1850 the then Anglican archdeacon of South Australia, Matthew Hale, established a mission on land at Poonindie, some 18 kilometres north of Port Lincoln. It was not intended for the locals, but to take young Aboriginal people away from more settled areas in the colony and place them in an isolated spot, where they could work the land

Poonindie, c. 1875. [SLSA B 43235]

and be transformed into 'good and useful' members of society. Perhaps inevitably, the removal plan was too ambitious, and in due course the mission became home to local people who, in spite of ups and downs, made a success of farming until the mission was abruptly sold off to white farmers in 1894.[13] These days all that remains of the Poonindie Mission is the famed Anglican 'church with a chimney'.

You can see the site from the Lincoln Highway, and read an excellent mission history written by Peggy Brock and Doreen Kartinyeri. And, as with the Lutheran Koonibba Mission established beyond Ceduna less than a decade after Poonindie's closure in 1894 (and several decades after pastoralists reached Ceduna), it seems that when the residents of Poonindie were dispersed, they were more likely to succeed in the outside world than those from beyond its walls due to the skills acquired at the mission.[14]

Elliston

Elliston, a small port located halfway up the west coast, is another key reference point in the story of Aboriginal people on Eyre Peninsula in the mid-19th century. Two things made it so. First and most importantly was the 'Elliston massacre' in 1849, the reality of which has been much disputed. The second is that Eyre Peninsula's only colonial writer of significance, Ellen Liston, worked there as a governess during this period. Apparently it is unclear as to whether the town is named after her, but her writings have been attracting some attention of late, and are very much of their time and place.[15]

Recent research into the Elliston massacre shows that the extension of the pastoral frontier up the west coast in the mid-19th century brought with it renewed violence and racial conflict. It also suggests that the story of a massacre at Elliston began to circulate some decades later, and cites possibly related instances of violence. Here it is I think best to quote Foster and Nettelbeck directly:

> If there is truth in these stories, its origins probably lie in the punitive expeditions which were organised not just in response to settlers' deaths but also for the minor attacks on local stations. Thomas Coper Horn led one such expedition three weeks after Easton's death [a shepherd's wife killed at nearby Lake Hamilton, when stores were also robbed] . . . Horn's party tracked the alleged offenders to the Waterloo Bay cliffs. As the Aborigines scrambled down the cliffs to escape, Horn and his men fired upon them, killing three and capturing five others.[16]

Evidently, the Elliston massacre story, long suppressed, was part of the cloak of secrecy that served to mask the violent reality of the settler frontier in supposedly peaceable South Australia. By now there is an array of oral testimony on the web from members of the Aboriginal community as to those violent realities, including the massacre, and it is said that Aboriginal people now steer well clear of Elliston because of its bad associations. Meanwhile, the town's possibly somewhat dubious notoriety has put it on the tourist map.

Ellen Liston (1838–1885), who arrived in South Australia from England in 1850, was a governess at Nilkerloo Station, inland from Streaky Bay, for five years, from 1867–1872, when she returned to Adelaide and a job in the post office. She later trained as a teacher. An independent-minded young woman, she enjoyed her years at Nilkerloo, and it was there that she began writing verse and short stories, some of which we can now see bear on her experience of Aboriginal people, albeit obliquely, as in the short story 'Doctor', written in 1882 and said to be her most powerful short fiction.[17]

Somewhat surprisingly, 'Doctor' turns out to be the name of a dog, a rather fierce dog at that. (Apparently dogs were often kept for protection against Aboriginal attacks.) In this narration, the dog Doctor saves a pastoralist's isolated wife Kit from an assault by Coomultie, an Aboriginal man. Kit has known that 'the blacks were numerous and oft-times troublesome' but the attack came when she was indoors and it takes her by surprise. Without the dog, she is sure she would not have survived. But it seems strange that she should know Coomultie's name, and that he enters her hut alone. In his chapter on the story, Rick Hosking suggests that Coomultie may have been known to her, and driven by hunger, as were many Aboriginal people on the Peninsula by the 1860s.

When in Liston's story Kit's husband returns, cursing the 'black devil', she is unable to re-enter the hut she had been staying in, and is weakened by pregnancy. Back at the station, she suffers a miscarriage; all becomes a blur; and she later learns that there had been many such assaults, resulting in 'a crusade against the natives' organised by 'a muster of hands from several stations' (cited Hosking, p. 70). There is little reason to doubt the reality of 'crusades'. Race relations on these far frontiers were almost entirely unregulated. The writer concludes: 'They [the crusaders] cannot be blamed, for we are too far from civilisation to depend on lawful redress, though without doubt many of the unoffending suffered with the guilty . . .'. Ultimately, somewhat haplessly perhaps, or maybe just realistically for the times, Liston makes allowances: 'But that is not a result confined to dealings of whites with blacks – it tells both ways'.[18]

How, and how many, Aboriginal people survived the pastoral era is hard, if not impossible, to determine. However, it was probably somewhat easier for them to do so then than in the agricultural period that followed. European-style farming on marginal land was hardly very profitable, but by the later 19th century it extended well into the saltbush country beyond Ceduna, leaving little space to the Wirangu and surrounding peoples.

What was left for them was some casual work, and from 1901 they had Koonibba, the Lutheran mission. Perhaps it should be noted by way of background that the Lutheran Church, a German church established by the 16th century by religious reformer Martin Luther, has been a presence in South Australia since the arrival of a dissident Prussian community in the 1840s, and has played a significant role in the founding of missions to Aboriginal people in the state. Maybe it was the strong discipline that the church maintained that enabled it to do so until well into the 20th century.

If you travel along Highway 1 west of Ceduna for some 40 kilometres, you will see a sign pointing north to Koonibba. I assumed we would need permission to visit but apparently not: there was no sign and we drove straight in. It was a privilege to do so. Remarkably, through ups and downs and in a much smaller area than originally, an Aboriginal community of some 150 residents has survived there to the present day, still predominantly Lutheran though no longer formally associated with the church, and now self-governing. The mission was first mooted in the late 1890s and up and running on a substantial site, with a resident pastor, support staff, a church, a school, a hospital, and a children's home, a decade or so later.[19]

The impact of Koonibba seems to be similar to that of Poonindie, only much stronger. Both 'push' and 'pull' factors worked to make it so. On the one hand, there was a need for a safe haven for the Aboriginal people of the Denial Bay area who had lost so much of their traditional territory by the beginning of the 20th century. This need was redoubled in the 1930s for Aboriginal people from the interior who were driven south by drought and the disruptions which followed the building of the transcontinental railway in preceding decades, and especially for Aboriginal children after the closure of the United Aboriginal Mission at Ooldea in 1934. On the other hand, the Lutheran mission had the lure of a lot more land than Poonindie, land that was farmed with varying degrees of success until the 1930s. Crucially, this meant jobs for adult males. As well, the mission had considerable success with their school and church, and as such fostered life-changing experiences for those seeking to understand change or simply enjoy new things. These days it is almost impossible to read an Aboriginal memoir of the region without hearing echoes of Koonibba.

It makes no sense to deny these historical realities. Of course, missions were far from perfect. As Peggy Brock has detailed in *Outback Ghettoes* (1993), many Aboriginal people found the Koonibba regime rigid and oppressive and left as soon as they could: only some people responded to or benefited from what the Lutherans had to offer. Moreover, such missions were few and far between, with limited resources and alien agendas. Nonetheless, for a time they probably did operate as a kind of pace-setter, especially for the men who did all the farm work, but also the women who served inside the oft-times quite substantial stone dwellings built for staff on the missions. It was not until the early 20th century that the state became a major determinant of the lives of Aboriginal people, and even then not much happened to change things.

As suggested earlier, the larger demographic story is one of a worsening situation. On the far west coast however, this may not have been quite the case. Certainly a century on, approximately one quarter of the 3500-strong population in the Ceduna Council area, which includes Koonibba, were of Aboriginal descent and Ceduna had one of the highest proportions of Aboriginal people in the state. No doubt it always did.[20]

Meanwhile, race was not something white settlers really thought about, unless they had to. They believed that, with luck, 'the black problem' would solve itself and, in the not necessarily vicious slogan, all that could be done was 'smooth the dying pillow'. That was what in effect Daisy Bates taught.

In her later years, when she was something of a grand dame, Bates was a peripheral figure in the life of the Peninsula, having moved her camp from the west to near Fowlers Bay in 1913, and five years later, inland to Ooldea on the transcontinental railway line, where she remained until 1935. She also passed through the region on trips east to conferences during those years. Later still, in the mid-1940s, she spent time at Streaky Bay, where she was an honoured presence among the settlers. But by then she was in her late eighties and a spent force so far as the welfare of Aboriginal people was concerned and mostly living in Adelaide. There in the late 1930s she had contributed to the Adelaide *Advertiser* and, with the help of writer Ernestine Hill published, *The Passing of the Aborigines* (1938), said by her most recent biographer Bob Reece to be 'one of the most influential books ever published in the English language', albeit in effect a retrograde influence due to her 'smooth the dying pillow' philosophy, which was even by then outdated. She died in Adelaide on 20 April 1951, aged 92. Whether any Aboriginal people mourned her passing is unknown. But it made headlines in the local press, and everyone knew of it.[21]

By then any anxiety about the fate of Aboriginal people on the west coast had passed or was suppressed. The situation was much the same on the east coast. The arrival of British colonisers at Franklin Harbour, midway along Spencer Gulf, in the 1850s meant more pastoralism, and similar conflict. *Saga of Wangaraleednie* captures some of it, including a public hanging of four Aboriginal men convicted of the murder of a shepherd in 1856.[22]

Few of the first peoples survived the establishment of small farming communities along the east coast and inland in the later 19th century. In *Saga of Wangaraleednie*, Masters writes regretfully of this, and offers a chilling account of the ending of one Tommy Momeuda, said to be 'the last of the tribes' in the area. According to Masters, Momeuda and his pack of half-starved dogs were one of the nuisances of the district, as the dogs invariably raided the settlers' meat stores. Even when Donald Young (a settler) hung a sheep's carcass too high for his own dogs to reach, Momeuda's dogs still managed to get to most of it, as Young found the next morning. Evidently, this was too much for Young. He baited the remaining meat and left it about in the evening. To this temptation the whole of Momeuda's pack succumbed.

Next morning Momeuda came to Young – 'Good-day, you Mr Young, goodbye' – and then let fly in his own dialect with threats on Young's head. However, Young understood the dialect and, as Masters tells it, to Momeuda's surprise, explained to him in the same tongue what had happened, finishing by lapsing into his usual Scottish brogue with 'it's God's truth, me mon'. Masters concludes his account as follows: 'Momeuda soon made himself scarce and got out of Donald's sight. Without his dogs he was more lonely than ever and shortly after gave up the ghost, and so passed the last specimen of civilised homicide' (p. 110).

No present-day writer would put it like that. Masters' account of the fate of Momeuda is a primary source in itself. Are there others like it? What else can be learned from court records and the local press? A good deal, of course. But it does seem that, compared with the west coast, less has survived on the historical record about these matters. A police presence was established up-country in the 1850s and at Cowell in the 1880s. If the police were anything like William Willshire, whose unsavoury career as officer-in-charge of the Native Police in Central Australia in the 1880s and 1890s ended at Cowell some 20 years later, this silence is not surprising. No doubt there were still 'quite a few'

Aboriginal people about when the Schiller family arrived in Cowell in 1907 but, apart from a wonderful horseman (unnamed), they had by then been reduced to 'a poor, harmless lot, dressed in rags', a matter of passing reference only. Moreover, apart from Poonindie in the south, no major Christian mission was established on the east coast in the colonial years or after. Thus by the 1950s the years of silence had well and truly set in. And by then no one, not even many of the widely dispersed Aboriginal people, were keen to revisit the past.[23]

The Stuart case

Then came another of those reality checks. On Friday 19 December 1958, Rupert Maxwell Stuart, an Aboriginal man born in Central Australia, arrived at Ceduna with a 'Funland' troupe. Next day, after apparently working a shift at the troupe's darts stand, and much drinking, he was arrested and later charged with the rape and murder of nine-year-old Mary Alice Hattam on a beach near Thevenard, and on 24 April 1959 he was convicted by a jury in Adelaide and sentenced to death, despite some serious problems of evidence. Stuart could neither read nor write and spoke only pidgin English, and his guilt rested almost entirely on a confession written in impeccable English by local police, who insisted the words were his. An execution was averted, but appeals to the Supreme Court of South Australia were unavailing and a subsequent appeal to the High Court of Australia was unsuccessful, despite some concerns expressed by the judges.[24]

Stuart's case was problematic from the start. It was first taken up by prison chaplain Father Tom Dixon, a Catholic priest who had worked in Central Australia and spoke Stuart's native Arrente, then by local anthropologists, especially Professor Ted Strehlow, who was brought up at Hermannsburg, and in short order by the press and staff and students at the University of Adelaide (of whom I was one). One of the early alerts that something was amiss came from a young history lecturer, Ken Inglis, who reported the doubts of Dixon and Strehlow in the fortnightly journal *Nation* (and delivered a memorable lunch hour lecture on the case when his book *The Stuart Case* [1961] was published – the place was packed out).

Father Dixon collected more evidence. The *Adelaide News*, then run by the young Rupert Murdoch, and the *Sydney Morning Herald* took up the cause, and concern was by then widespread. But the Playford government was unflinching, especially when an appeal to the Privy Council in London failed. Ultimately, a royal commission forced its hand, and Stuart's death sentence was commuted to a life sentence. Thereafter Stuart was in and out of jail several times until finally released in the 1980s and soon after became an elder in the Arrernte community south-east of Alice Springs. There he married and became a respected figure. Kwementyaye Stuart, as he became known, died in November 2014.[25]

Almost two generations have passed since the Stuart case and it may seem it has been quite forgotten. But there was a powerful feature film about it in 2002 called *Black and White*, and it surely is not forgotten by Aboriginal people, nor by the older residents of South Australia, many of whom protested strongly about its conduct at the time. Moreover it has left a definite imprint on Australian history. The case bore directly on the move away from 'assimilation' to 'integration' in South Australia in the later 1960s led by the young Don Dunstan. It was doubtless a factor in the success of the campaign by Jessie Street, Faith Bandler, and others which led to the referendum in 1967. This gave the Commonwealth (part) responsibility for Aboriginal affairs and enabled the counting of Aboriginal people in the census.

Through a glass darkly

By 1974 the Commonwealth had assumed full responsibility for Aboriginal affairs (except in Queensland). This was a major step forward and impacted on the lives of Aboriginal people everywhere. The almost 150 years of state responsibility in South Australia seemed to be over. But there were still all sorts of ambiguities and overlaps at state level, as with housing and education, and Eyre Peninsula is still a long way from legislative reach. Meanwhile, with the decline of smaller towns, in many places there is no longer an Aboriginal presence. Like everyone else, they have congregated in the larger towns.[26]

There are two sides to most stories, including the story of survival. Even by 1913 some statisticians doubted that Aboriginal people were dying out in South Australia and, inadequate as the pre-1967 statistics are, it was evident by the 1940s that their number in the settled areas of the state was increasing, if slowly. How this trend applied to a late-developing region like Eyre Peninsula is unclear – in accordance with public policy, my own relatives were still taking up land in the Wudinna area in the 1920s – but the Aboriginal population was always thinly spread, and by then farming had taken over much of the interior. Thus it is by no means a straightforward or balanced story: a realistic assessment of the situation by the early 20th century would surely be that conflict over land on the Peninsula was effectively over, and that in consequence attitudes were changing.

Tracing changes in attitudes is seldom easy. Cultural change is usually slow. Speaking for myself, the first really positive sign came in art classes. I have mentioned these already, but now I should pay further tribute to Miss Clarkson, the art teacher, who first introduced my class to Aboriginal art. It was not only Rex Battarbee's book on the subject but also the work of Albert Namatjira that captured our interests. His colours were much brighter than anything nearby but, as with the Maralinga tests, the paintings felt as if they were from our part of the world.[27]

Of one thing we may be sure. Although we see but through a glass darkly now, there will be more change to come. Inevitably it is ongoing. And again the indicators are mixed. When people think about the situation of Aboriginal people out west these days, more often than not the first thing that comes to mind is the problem of grog, the problem that caused so much trouble for Eddie Betts, Albert Namatjira and Max Stuart. As recently as 23 April 2013 the *Australian* newspaper carried a report of high blood alcohol levels among Aboriginal men entering the local sobering-up shelter at Ceduna and calls for government intervention and income management. According to the president of the Ceduna Business and Tourism Association, Greg Limbert, the situation will only get worse if nothing is done. It puts the tourists off: '[t]he problem is physical violence. It's alcohol-based fighting. It's the way they're walking down the road soliciting tourists for money. There are a whole host of things going on.'

In retrospect, we may catch glimpses of cultural changes that have aided as well as abetted survival in the 20th century. There were, and are, still two classes of citizens, but some improvements too, for instance in education, as with some interesting interactions among schoolchildren. Lois Healy, a teacher-librarian at Kirton Point Primary in the 1970s, has recalled student camping trips during the school year where Aboriginal students' skills shone out. Likewise, students at Port Lincoln High School conducted their own researches into local cultures in the 1980s. Alongside such extra-curricula activities, I'm told there have also been enhancements to the curriculum that will be of long-run benefit.[28]

Looked at on a broader scale, schooling for young Aboriginal people remains a concern. How serious a concern is something to be explored further. A similar story might be told of health, including mental health. And how are women and girls faring? There seems to be a lamentable silence when it comes to gender analysis. Here I think of Eddie Betts's daughter, who went down to Port Lincoln police station on that last day of his life to try to help him but it was too late. His fate tells us that survival is not enough.

CHAPTER 10

Since the 1960s

continuity and change – the towns – the weekends – north/south – events – the 2005 bushfire – Gallipoli – what next? – holidays and tourism – some prominent people – people and place

'What state is Spencer Gulf part of?' Imagine my surprise to find this as the first question in the *Sydney Morning Herald*'s Saturday *Spectrum* quiz. An easy one for me of course, but for how many other *Herald* readers, I wondered. Our newspapers and our cultures are firmly state-based, and the states with smaller populations like South Australia seldom attract wider media attention, much less the regions that make up those states. Admittedly, the 'region' is not the most exciting concept. There's no denying, however, that it works quite well for much of South Australia, and especially for Eyre Peninsula. In this last chapter, I attempt to pinpoint some of the main social and cultural changes on the Peninsula since my day.

My most recent trip to Eyre Peninsula occurred in October 2013. This 2013 trip, with colleagues David Carment, a leading historian of Northern Australia, and scholar-librarian Baiba Berzins, whose late husband Peter Loveday spent his early years near Streaky Bay, took us as far west as Penong and culminated at the centenary of the Yallunda Flat Show, held as usual on the Monday of the long weekend in October, with some 5000 people in attendance. The centenary was celebrated the preceding day with the launching of a professionally produced history of Yallunda Flat in the new wing of the showground's sheep-shearing shed, where I was pleased to be invited to say a few words, mainly about my father as founder of the sheep-shearing competition when he was president of the Show Committee in the 1950s.

Continuity and change

Like the rest of rural Australia, Eyre Peninsula would change considerably, if slowly, and maybe not always for the better, in the second half of the 20th century.

My father liked to reflect from time to time on the changes he'd seen during his life on the land. One story that sticks in my mind pertains to the impact of mechanisation. In the days of his youth, even quite modest farms employed at least one unskilled labourer, who often lived on site. By the 1950s, however, with the coming of tractors and other farm machinery, this would be more or less a thing of the past, except on large pastoral holdings such as the one where my stepbrother Ian briefly worked at Calca, south of Streaky Bay (an area now better known for whale watching). There were also occasional casual jobs such as scrub clearing, the latter a reminder of Larry and Terry – I never knew their surnames – who lived in a tent up in the hills at Kooltana and called by on weekends to flirt with my sisters.

Farming was not the only area where change was to become noticeable by the 1960s. Whereas many of those who built the railway lines and installed the water pipes moved on when the job was done, others, such as the railway workers whose stories are captured by Peter and Margaret Knife in *Peninsula Memories* (2007), stayed on to work, mostly in the towns. There were even a few mainly single men from the national post-World War II immigration program to be seen in the town streets by then.

Likewise, as the sorry story of Eddie Betts highlights, the Indigenous Australian population was increasingly drawn to the towns in the second half of the 20th century, the men in search of work on the docks and the roads. Some found toeholds in local economies and stayed put, but others were forced to move on when the jobs disappeared. As always with Indigenous history, the full story is yet to emerge; the lucky ones were probably those who were good at sport. At least we started to refer to Aboriginal people more respectfully about then, that is with a capital A, though it would take considerably longer for the word Indigenous to take hold.[1]

Overall, it seems that the population of the Eyre Peninsula region has stood at about 80,000 since the 1960s. When it comes to underlying trends, however, the available statistics are not easy to read. This is largely because the census figures on which our understanding depends are not collected on a regional basis, but in accordance with local government boundaries. As well, those boundaries change from time to time and some parts of the far north remain unincorporated. Nor is it easy to determine the balance of losses and gains over time. On the one hand, in some places there have been significant losses of population, most notably Whyalla, where the resident population fell from 33,000 in the 1970s to less than 22,000 at the 2011 census. On the other hand, gains from the national immigration program and the high levels of social mobility in this country are presumably of some significance. It does seem, however, that, even including estimates of the number of Indigenous people in unincorporated areas, the overall population of the Peninsula has seldom, if ever, surpassed 80,000 and that, on balance, the figures for loss and gain over time have not varied greatly. Together they point to considerable continuities. Nonetheless, as in the instances I've just cited, it is not hard to detect signs of social and cultural change.[2]

The towns

In Eyre Peninsula history, as elsewhere in the story of Australian country life, the towns have been a largely neglected dynamic. In the 19th century there were only a few towns on the Peninsula, all of them coastal, most of them with long jetties built in the late 19th or early 20th centuries. The main ones up the east coast were Port Lincoln, Tumby Bay, and Cowell, and along the much rougher west coast, Elliston, Streaky Bay and Ceduna, and they all remained significant throughout the 20th century. However, closer settlement and the coming of the rail in the early 20th century saw the creation of numerous inland towns as well, the larger ones being Cummins, Minnipa, and Kimba, all railway towns of some significance. Numerous smaller centres were established at that time too, although, as with Yallunda Flat when its general store closed in the late 1970s, they seldom survived far into the second half of the 20th century.

More recent developments have added a new and maybe perturbing dimension to the urban theme. Except for the industrial city of Whyalla, which did not get off the ground until the 1940s, most towns were always there as service centres, the larger ones with shops and banks and post offices, schools and churches and community halls. But there are now fewer such service centres. As travel by car has become easier, due to cheaper petrol and a much needed improvement of roads, and as e-services have become increasingly available, fewer local and community stores are needed, the larger towns have become more important, and the always comparatively close relationship between 'Adelaide and the country' has become closer. Until quite recently the big days in all the towns were the mail days – when the boats came in, when the trains delivered the mail to up-country sidings, when the mailman came along the bumpy roads, and later, when the buses arrived from Adelaide. Nowadays 'the mail' is not what it used to be and it is harder, if not impossible, for smaller places to keep going. By now it is nothing for people to drive from quite distant parts to Port Lincoln or Whyalla to shop, or to Tumby Bay for recreation, not to mention flights to Adelaide for the day from as far west as Ceduna for such things as specialist medical appointments.

To some extent, for the growth of towns, the period since the 1960s has been one of 'comers and goers'. While many of the 'comers' did become town-dwellers, others – in what proportion it would be impossible to say – would be 'goers', moving on either looking for work or according to the needs of the organisations they represented. Thus many of the teachers and clergy, the bank mangers and postmasters, the doctors and the nurses, hotel owners and the like, were 'goers', who came and went having enriched the communities they served, and are for the most part remembered with affection, not least as sportspeople. I have no trouble recalling the cavalcade of teachers who were appointed to the tiny one-teacher school at Yallunda Flat in my time, especially the greatly loved Mr Pengilly. Heather Bessen, who was much younger, captained the 'A' grade basketball team and could dance the quickstep.

In an earlier chapter, some of the passing clergy are also recalled, such as the Methodist (now Uniting) Church minister Mr Forth, whose sermon on 'the green light' for some now un-retrievable reason has stuck in my mind, and the high Anglican priest, the Reverend Alexander Macintosh, whose untimely death in 1949 was to indirectly affect the course of my life by bringing me a stepmother. Some of the male teachers became local preachers too, a memorable example being David Floyd Smith, who later became a distinguished agricultural scientist at Melbourne University, and was the inaugural teacher of 'Ag Science' at Cummins Area School when I was there. Some women teachers taught in the Sunday schools in the larger towns too (as would many girls of my generation but not me; Yallunda Flat was too small for that).

It seems health professionals were not so mobile. Doctors needed to be near hospitals, of which there were six or more on the Peninsula by the late 20th century, not only in the larger towns at or near the coast but also smaller centres up-country such as Wudinna. The highly esteemed Dr Wibberley of Tumby Bay, who was said to have been a Christian socialist, stayed for years, as did the colourful Dr Trudinger at Elliston, where the locals erected a memorial park in his honour in 1966. I paid my respects to it when passing through in 2007 (a colleague at Macquarie is one of his granddaughters). I also checked that Dr Wibberley's impressive two-storied house-cum-surgery was still standing by the Tumby Bay foreshore during that trip. In such company it would hardly be fair to recall the general practitioner at a nearby town who was alleged to drink too much.

Nurses probably moved about more, presumably to gain further experience and higher qualifications than could be obtained in small country hospitals. My mother Edna Heath's time as a nurse began at Wudinna in the 1920s. Later, she moved to Adelaide, where she trained at the Royal Adelaide, prior to marriage back home in 1933. In the mid-1950s her oldest daughter, Pauline, went straight to Adelaide to train at the Adelaide Children's Hospital, and remained in the city as a health professional after marriage.

The weekends

Country people came into town during the week to collect the mail and to shop. On the weekends they came for enjoyment, especially on Saturdays, for sport in the afternoon and, in the larger centres – before the coming of television – for 'the pictures' or a dance in the town hall at night. In between the two, there would be a meal in a local café, consisting of roast meat and two veg or a mixed grill, and a cup of tea or coffee, the latter made from Bushells Coffee Essence and condensed milk. It may not seem much of a treat now, but for us at least, Saturday lunch usually consisted of boiled meat and sago – it was thought important to avoid fatty foods before sport – so it probably seemed quite glamorous.

Even now it would be hard to imagine life in the country without sport. Indeed it sometimes seems as if country communities are basically sustained by sport, and that sport is a kind of religion there. Certainly over time all the main sports have attracted players and supporters in numbers on Eyre Peninsula and, for some, organised sport has been the high road to status and esteem. The most striking examples have been with Indigenous men, such as Dick Davey, who began playing football at Koonibba aged 14 in about 1906 and is said to have played all over the Peninsula with 'brilliance and courage'.[3] For such men, it has been *A Kind of Magic*, the title of a thorough compilation of Aboriginal achievements in Australian Rules football on Eyre Peninsula by John Gascoyne published in 2006. Maybe some

Indigenous girls have done well in sport too, but their names are not easily recalled, in part because of the lower esteem in which women's sport has been held.

Team sports offer the best evidence of sport as a force for continuity and community in the country. It was true of football and basketball in winter, cricket and tennis in summer. Perhaps team sports were more sociable, with competitive sport on Saturdays and sport for relaxation on Sundays, after church in our case. When bowls were introduced in the 1950s, they were immediately popular with older players, offering the opportunity both to acquire new skills and to enjoy congenialities from the sidelines throughout the week. Whether or not being fully decked out in white is still *de rigeur*, bowls itself remains popular, unlike croquet, another once popular game played by both men and women, but by the 1950s, by just a few older women.

So far as the young were concerned, the best moment was probably the interval between the two pictures shown on most Saturday nights, when there would be just enough time to rush out to a nearby cafe for refreshments: maybe an Eskimo Pie (a chocolate-coated ice cream marketed in Australia by Peters) or a soft drink of some kind (pre-Coke, probably lemonade from the local soft drink company, Port Lincoln Springs). And, with luck, there'd still be time for a cuddle with one of the boys behind the hall loos on the way back. Behind the scenes within the hall there would be a ticket seller and projectionist, but the young gave little, if any, thought to these responsible adults, or indeed to the venues, usually quite modest town halls owned by local councils.

A similar story might be told about the dances held in those same town halls. Once upon a time there were even occasional dances at the Yallunda Flat Hall, although the tiny community could not sustain a regular picture show. For many people in that era, wherever they were, a dance was the week's highlight, and considerable distances would be traversed, even in the days of horse-drawn transport, to enjoy them. A local musical group, consisting of at least a pianist and a drummer, would provide the music; a local Master of Ceremonies would announce the dances in a big voice; and the women seated demurely around the hall would wait to be invited to take to the floor. Mostly the men huddled at the back of the hall before making a rush for a partner, although some would also trickle in from outside, as they certainly did when 'the Alberts' were announced. 'The Alberts' were a kind of square dance, and supper (alcohol-free) always followed. It would all be over by midnight, but it was nothing for dancers to get home at two o'clock the next morning. On the downside, the cows would be waiting at the usual hour to be milked.

These days country people are more likely to be at home watching television in the evenings, and to buy their milk at whatever times the shops are open. But there is not much to suggest that a commitment to organised sport on the weekends is weakening, although it too revolves around the towns. Where the smaller settlements have declined, so too have the sporting facilities. At Chandada, inland from Streaky Bay, which I saw in October 2013, the local hall remains quite impressive but the adjacent oval is no longer in use. Nor, apparently, are the basketball courts at Yallunda Flat.

North/south

The increasing importance of the north of the Peninsula is a theme touched upon several times in preceding pages, starting with the early east–west truck driver, the young Ray Gilleland. When the section of the Eyre Highway which runs across the north of the Peninsula was finally bitumenised in the 1970s, Kimba and Wudinna benefited as the main fuel stops between Port Augusta and Ceduna, as did tourism to the Gawler Ranges National Park, which can be reached from Wudinna or Minnipa in the west or from Kimba to the south-west.

It is not so much that the population up north has increased significantly or that many new industries have taken hold, but rather that the profile of the north has been lifted by comers and goers and by the development of pre-existing industries like fishing at Ceduna. In addition, residents from surrounding areas have increasingly retired to the coastal towns, as was apparent to me at Venus Bay on the upper west coast and again at Port Neill, to the north of Tumby Bay, in 2013.

Less apparent, but known to me on a personal basis and worth mentioning ,have been movements interstate. How many went I could not say, but members of the Heath family who moved to Dalwallinu on Western Australia's wheat belt in the late 1950s and a family from Stokes near Yallunda Flat who moved to the wide open spaces of northern New South Wales a decade or so later have stayed in my mind, as have all those old farmers and their wives who took to spending their winters on Queensland's central coast in the late 1960s and early 1970s. John Roe and his second wife Jane were among them.

Events

Arguably the region has become more widely known since the 1950s. Now big events on Eyre Peninsula are as likely as not to make the national news but, apart from the visit by the young Queen Elizabeth II and her consort the Duke of Edinburgh to Whyalla and Port Lincoln in early 1954, the Redex car reliability trials of the mid-1950s were probably the first events to do so. Promoted by a car lubricant salesman, these trials, as described by Phil Matthews, were billed as 'the biggest, toughest, longest, richest, and most dramatic in history' and, although intermittent thereafter and, in effect, superseded by the Bathurst races in the late 1960s, they were a big excitement at the time. In the second trial in mid-1954, which was the first all-round Australia trial, the road that crossed the Peninsula from Ceduna to Port Augusta was there on the map in the national press for all to see. But the drivers were reportedly tired by then – the route took them anti-clockwise from Sydney – and it was a rough section, with rain after Ceduna: 'the tired cars and crews had to battle their way through long stretches of mud' (*Redex to Repco*, p. 54). Not surprisingly, few participants had much to say about that stretch.

The local press was much more expansive. For the *Port Lincoln Times* there was news aplenty. The frightful state of the roads was a topic close to their readers' hearts, as were the cars, especially perhaps the car driven by eventual winner 'Gelignite Jack' Murray, who drove a Ford V8 in 1954. Country people were keen drivers and they preferred American to British cars. For women readers, the *Australian Women's Weekly* had more coverage. Women drivers entered the trials from the beginning, despite male antipathy. Probably the best known was the intrepid 65-year-old Winifred Conway of Rose Bay, Sydney, who learned to drive in 1913. In 1954 the *Weekly* entered its own four-woman team, with the well-known journalist Helen Frizell as captain-navigator. They had a great time in their Humber Super Snipe and, as it happened, they were the only all-woman crew to complete the course. Although there is no actual evidence of it, we may be sure that the women of Eyre Peninsula read every word of Frizell's reports in the *Weekly*.[4]

The all-female *Australian Women's Weekly* Redex team on the cover of the magazine, 7 July 1954.

That was 1954. In late 1959 came the Stuart case. As mentioned previously, it was the *Sydney Morning Herald* that brought the Stuart case to national attention, and the ensuing indignation at the treatment Stuart received from the forces of law and order at Ceduna and subsequently from the Playford government in Adelaide was widely reported. The same cannot be said for the Betts case, though it was given considerable attention in the Aboriginal Deaths in Custody inquiry in the 1990s. Since then no comparable cases have arisen and Indigenous issues seem to have faded from wider view, except at Ceduna, where the higher proportion of unsettled Aboriginal people in the town ensures that problematic race relations are apparent to all, including tourists.

What does unfailingly draw wider attention are successes in major sporting events, and natural disasters. Even I, in far-off Sydney, paid attention when a Port Lincoln horse Makybe Diva won the Melbourne Cup in 2004. Makybe Diva belonged to Tony Santic, a millionaire tuna fisherman of Croation origin in Port Lincoln. You can see a life-size statue of the horse in a park on the inner foreshore at Port Lincoln.

The 2005 bushfire

Winning the Melbourne Cup was an astonishing sporting triumph. Not long after came a shocking natural disaster. On Tuesday 11 January 2005, a major bushfire swept across Lower Eyre Peninsula, causing nine deaths, four of them of children, numerous casualties, and huge stock losses, as well as significant losses of housing and of infrastructure such as fencing and water mains. The estimated cost overall would run to millions of dollars.

The 2005 fire, the biggest in South Australia since 'Ash Wednesday' burnt through the Adelaide Hills in 1983, was widely reported on national television and in the press. To my astonishment and concern, there would even be a map on page three of the *Sydney Morning Herald* on the Thursday with Yallunda Flat marked on it, so far as I know the first such notice since the footrace in the film *Gallipoli* (1981) was shot on the picturesque showground.

Apparently the fire started in roadside vegetation near the small township of Wangary, some 45 kilometres north-west of Port Lincoln, shortly after 3 pm on Monday 10 January. At the time, no one seemed sure what caused it. But with bushfires there is always a cause, often a complex one, and usually one in which humans play a significant part, a point most recently stressed in an insightful memoir of the catastrophic fires in Victoria in 2009 entitled *Gardens of Fire* (2013) by historian Robert Kenny, who lost his home near Bendigo to the fires. Later it emerged in the course of a coronial inquiry that the fire on Lower Eyre Peninsula had been caused by a spark from the exhaust of a Toyota 4WD owned by Marco Visic of Port Lincoln, a would-be gold prospector who was checking possible sites in the area at that time. There would also be controversy over the response to the Monday flare-up. Some thought that the Country Fire Service reacted too slowly and that it should have used aerial bombardment at that stage. Against this charge, the volunteer firefighters defended themselves vigorously in the local press. This too was thoroughly investigated by the Coroner. The inquiry would find many inadequacies in the initial response to the fire.[5]

According to the defensive scenario, the fire got away more or less unimpeded, to wreak havoc once it reached the small town of Wanilla, west of Port Lincoln – which, however inadequate that scenario proved to be to an understanding to the course of events, it certainly did. On the following day, Tuesday 11 January, the fire swept eastward over the Koppio Hills to reach the small towns at the northern end of Boston Bay. Nine people died due to the fire: two firefighters and a grandmother and her two grandchildren at Wanilla, a mother and her two children at Poonindie and another woman at North Shields. It was there that, due to a wind change, the fire turned northwards, to reach almost as far as Tumby Bay, and then north-west, to about halfway to Yallunda Flat from Tumby, it reached as far north as the Bratten Highway, which runs east–west from Tumby Bay through Yallunda Flat to Cummins and beyond. There, on Wednesday 12 January, it was halted. The Flat, as it was often called, was lucky to escape, and so was the Koppio Smithy Museum, saved by the firefighters, and 'the church with a chimney' at Poonindie.

Of the fire in its later stages and its aftermath, some wonderful photographs were taken by press photographers: of burnt out hills where all that was left was ash and stumps and dead trees, of exhausted volunteer fire fighters, and of the path of the fire itself. Everywhere, it was reported, the emergency services were at full stretch, and it seems there could never be enough praise for the helpers behind the scenes. Only one instance of looting was reported. Likewise, that stoicism which I recall so well as an aspect of rural life – you must never feel sorry for yourself – was much in evidence. My favourite quote from the extended coverage of the fire in the *Port Lincoln Times* in January 2005 came from 81-year-old Lorna Harding of North Shields, who lost everything, including her family home adjacent to the North Shields jetty: 'We won't be the first and we won't be the last . . . The sun will come up again tomorrow morning'. In due course the paper would be full of community efforts to support the firefighters (who came from all over the state and some beyond), and then to help with clean up.

> Rebuilding Lower Eyre Peninsula with the brow sweat of people from the farming community along with city volunteers will not only help reduce the time to rebuild, it will also build stronger community ties.[6]

In this context, mention should also be made of the role of the state government in coping with the fire and its aftermath. It may be too big a subject to pursue here but, as elsewhere in the region's history – for example in the building of jetties and railways – state support for recovery and rebuilding was vital.

In *Burning Bush: A fire history of Australia* (1991), a pioneering history of bushfires in this country, American fire historian Stephen J. Pyne marks Eyre Peninsula out as the western tip of 'a colossal fire flume' of continental significance: '[t]hree points – Eyre Peninsula, Botany Bay, Port Phillip Bay – inscribe the great fire triangle of Australia' (p. 50). This may sound rather grand, but the 'Black Tuesday' bushfire of 2005 was a disaster, and it is a reminder that Eyre Peninsula is a part of the driest state in Australia, which is, in turn, the driest continent in the world, and that bushfires always have a cause. Moreover, even in the drier north of the region they seem to be occurring more frequently, as with the recent fires in the semi-arid Gawler Ranges, due, it may be, to increasing tourist traffic. At the time of writing, total fire bans were in place for much of the Peninsula (the west coast, eastern Eyre Peninsula and Lower Eyre Peninsula). Even in late April the threat of fire in those parts was deemed severe.

Gallipoli

Eyre Peninsula may seem an unlikely place for making films. However, the making of films was a major South Australian endeavour in the late 20th century and, as it happens, the Peninsula provided a suitable site for one of Australia's most famous films. Filmmaker Peter Weir had wanted to make a film about Gallipoli for a long time and, with writer David Williamson, had spent some five years working a script. But it was a big and costly project and, as producer Patricia Lovell tells it in her autobiography *No Picnic* (1995), it took a lot of effort to obtain funding, in the end from Robert Stigwood and Rupert Murdoch, both wealthy expatriates, and it was not until the late 1970s that the project got off the ground. Soon after, on a flight in a light aircraft over Eyre Peninsula, Weir and actor Mark Lee found 'an ideal location to re-create Anzac Cove' (p. 218), some 50 kilometres north-west of Port Lincoln, at an isolated spot to the north of Coffin Bay then known as Farm Beach.

Lovell admits that she was taken aback when she learned that there was only a dirt track into Farm Beach from the Flinders Highway and that they would have to build a proper road to get all the necessary equipment in, but it was not that far and they managed. They were happy with the Flinders Highway, and with their quarters in Port Lincoln. Apparently members of the production staff were located in the city for as long as six months, working from an unused part of the fish canning company Safcol's freezers unit.

Several sources emphasise that the most demanding part of the filming at Farm Beach was with the trenches constructed on the cliff face. At some stages, many more extras were needed, but there was

Farm Beach transformed into Anzac Cove (left) and filming in 'the trenches' on Eyre Peninsula. [Associated R&R Films]

no problem about that as it was the off-season in the tuna fishing industry and filming at Farm Beach coincided with the end of the school year, which meant that students over the age of 16 could also be recruited. Thus my sister Jean's son Stanley, who was not quite 17 at the time, was one of some 200 extras to be bussed in daily during the fortnight it took to shoot the main scenes: the landing, the charge over the trenches, and the subsequent fall back. In an interview for this book, Stanley recalled being paid for what must have been an exciting time, and that they all had to have 1915 haircuts.[7]

The previously mentioned Yallunda Flat Showground, where the foot race at the beginning of *Gallipoli* was shot is probably the locality's only wider claim to fame.

When the film was released in 1981, there was a special showing at Port Lincoln. Peter 'Kiwi' White was there and recalls a huge 'buzz' in the theatre as people recognised the scenes and some of the players. Those scenes at Farm Beach and Yallunda Flat Showground are probably largely forgotten even there by now, but they stand alongside the royal visit in the cultural history of Eyre Peninsula.

What next?

At first glance, it may seem that droughts would have brought a wider attention to Eyre Peninsula. They have occurred with comparable frequency to bushfires, and can be the source of considerable distress. However, it seem historians have had little to say on the subject and, having spent most of my childhood in the milder, wetter south, I don't have much by way of experience to draw on. Mainly what comes to mind is anxious talk up Wudinna way. Perhaps this – to me – unexpected silence is because drought, which simply means a severe lack of water, is somehow less dramatic than bushfire, more the proverbial 'Act of God', and there is nothing much to be done about it except conserve what water there is and hang in until it rains.

Far more attention-grabbing developments may be in store. It has been mentioned in passing that Eyre Peninsula sits at the southern edge of Gondwana. Readers will also be aware that in Western Australia there is an ancient plateau rich in iron ore deposits. The possibility that this might also be the case in the east has not escaped investors. Although it is neither easy nor in this context necessary to predict future developments, it is well known that practically the entire east coast from beyond Buckleboo and Kimba as far south as Koppio has been surveyed by mining interests and found to contain reserves of hematite, and that plans for a new port north of Tumby Bay, previously called Sheep Hill, now Port Spencer, are well advanced, with a new railway line projected linking the proposed port to the eastern arm of the existing system at Ungarra. Indeed, so hopeful have investors been that by 2013 there were three ports projected by mining interests between Tumby Bay and Cowell: in addition to the southernmost Sheep Hill/Port Spencer port some 20 kilometres from Tumby, there's another planned a little further north at Cape Hardy, 7 kilometres south of Port Neill, and a third at Lucky Bay, just beyond Cowell. The sites may not be very impressive, but the length of the proposed jetties shown on the websites certainly is.

Local opinion seems to be divided as to the proposed mining projects. Some think it's a bit old hat and the deposits are not rich enough to lead to much, and it does seem three ports would be excessive. Others think mining is inevitable, and to be welcomed as it would bring new life and opportunity to the whole region. With the high

Ports have always played an important role in Eyre Peninsula. Here MV *Minnipa* unloads a car onto the wharf at Port Lincoln, 1929.
[SLSA B71790/2]

capitalisation required, and the need to build new railways, only time will tell. Considering that there has been very little by way of mining in the region apart from the Middleback Ranges west of Whyalla, and the much smaller talc mining enterprises at Cowell and earlier near Tumby Bay, the locals have had little enough direct experience of what large-scale mining would mean for them. However, there is plenty of evidence from elsewhere in Australia, for instance the Hunter Valley in NSW, and it seems unlikely that a consensus will emerge.

Holidays and tourism

For many people it won't be the dramatic events but their own immediate encounters with the Peninsula that are the most telling. The days when Helen Bartley's father took his family cross-country to sleep in the wheat sheds at Venus Bay for their summer holidays have long since passed. But fishing remains a popular pastime, with all those wide beaches, low headlands, calm bays and swampy estuaries – Tumby Bay has the lot – and an array of edible saltwater fish to be caught, most memorably for me, whiting and tommy ruff.

By now there's a new, more luxurious dimension to recreation and holiday-making, with a grand new hotel on the Port Lincoln foreshore – quite near Grandmother Roe's house that amazingly is still there – and lavish fish and chips are served in the larger motel dining rooms to cater to the better off holiday-makers throughout. It is no exaggeration to say that these days there are holiday lettings at motels and caravan parks at all the main beaches. Evidently fishing and tourism have become major industries. Who would have thought in the 1950s that Port Lincoln with its tuna fishing fleets would become the biggest fishing port in Australia, or that the grandeur of the western coastline would be so assiduously promoted in the travel literature and so widely appreciated. The ever-widening appeal of Coffin Bay from a holiday-fishing village to a national resort may have been predictable, but whale watching at Baird Bay is something else, as is swimming in (protected) tanks with sharks down south. Even the interior has to some extent benefited from a more prosperous and mobile population, especially the Gawler Ranges, which may be accessed from Minnipa as well as from Whyalla, via tour companies promoting comforts past imagining.

A publicity photo promoting Port Lincoln's beach culture, c. 1974.
[SLSA B 53407/106]

Some prominent people

It is probably the case that individuals are just as significant as events and tourism in generating a profile for the region. Champion tennis player and later national coach John Fitzgerald is a conspicuous example. He came originally from Cockaleechie, just north of Yallunda Flat. Several other names spring to mind: Diana Howlett, a Ceduna-born geography professor in Canberra, now retired; the late Peter Loveday, a political scientist who started out at Chandada, near Streaky Bay; Frank Crowley, a distinguished professor of Australian history whose father was a clergyman at Streaky who died recently aged 88, and Peter Stanley, a prolific war historian in Canberra whose book on Whyalla in the 1940s I referred to earlier. The eminent CSIRO scientist Ivan Gentry Garrett was born at Tumby Bay in 1914, but the family left when he was five.

One prominent woman my stepmother felt I should know was Mrs Janet Octoman of Lipson, one of the few women from the region (along with the bus driver Mrs Birdseye) to make it into the *Australian Dictionary of Biography*. Mrs Octoman, who died in 1971, was a member of the Liberal Country Party who sought party nomination to the state parliament several times in vain, and became a national leader of the CWA. It was good to meet her, but she was a bit grand for me, and my schoolgirl aspirations did not include joining the CWA, admirable as its work has been. Hers is one of the graves to be visited at the Lipson cemetery. More recently, a few Indigenous women have attained prominence, as has Mercy Glastonbury in *Mazin Grace*.

Obviously these are all names of individuals drawn largely from my sort of world, the world of women and of academe. No doubt other writers would nominate others, from other areas of life. It is, however, unlikely that a full list of those who left ('the goers') would be long compared with the number of those who did not ('the stayers'). As for me, by now I seem to have fallen somewhere in between.

People and place

In setting out on this project, I had in mind only that it was a case of better late than never for a kind of family history, one set in a wider historical context. But I soon realised that there was more to it. Eyre Peninsula is not only one of the last areas of closer settlement, but also one of the oldest regions in Australia. It is both daunting and exciting to think that the place I come from reaches way back to the

Tuna fishing remains an important industry.
A tuna boat in Port Lincoln, c. 1974.
[SLSA B 53407/108]

fragmentation of the ancient super continent known as Gondwana.

Paradoxically, the faces that have been newest to me have been of those whose forebears have been on the Peninsula for the longest time, that is the Aboriginal people. It seems there have never been many of them on the Peninsula and, compared with the four-billion-year time span of Gondwana, they have not been there very long, the most recent estimates being maybe 50,000 years. The Nawu occupied the region I know best, but by my time, there had been considerable relocations. The Betts family, for example, were originally from way up north, from the Lutheran mission beyond Ceduna, so they were not Nawu.

Perhaps it is not surprising that my first research project was on Eyre Peninsula. Entitled 'A geographic field study of the hundreds of "Hutchison" and "Koppio", Eyre Peninsula, South Australia', happily I still have it – now a faded document in a black-covered exercise book. It doesn't mention Gondwana: the term itself had not yet become widely used or understood. Nor do the Nawu appear in the project. It would be some time before we took care to learn and differentiate the original inhabitants.

It is quite startling to look through the field study now. It's more like a small book! There are some 130 pages. Almost half is text, handwritten, of course, in pen and ink, amounting to maybe 15,000 words, and there is an array of graphics: numerous maps and diagrams, also hand-drawn, several pages of drawings and pressings of native flora, some 50 photographs (taken with a box Brownie), plus a few clippings from local newspapers, even a handwritten list of the first pupils at Yallunda Flat Primary School, provided by one of them.

'The purpose of this study', we are told on page two, 'is to describe the general conditions of climate, structure, vegetation, soils, topography, drainage, and other physical features which reveal the local diversity and interest of such conditions, then to show the effects and results of settlement upon this particular environment and describe the way of life existing there. The emphasis on human activity, and the changing methods of farming, will become obvious as the scene unfolds.'

It has taken me a long time to return to the subject, longer still to revisit my school project. As this chapter shows, by now both people and place have changed in various ways since the 1960s. But some things don't change that much. After a tense beginning in the

1840s, Eyre Peninsula became a stable and mostly prosperous place, with productive primary industries, modern service centres, and good communications. Meanwhile, as with my school project, the environment remains a basic concern, and cultural institutions such as the schools and churches are still vital to the health of communities. This book represents a mature foray into the story of Eyre Peninsula, this time with the benefits of professional training and experience. I trust it rings true to both people and place, and that it may serve to encourage fresh approaches to regional history.

NOTES

Chapter 1 ~ Getting there

1 Map of Aboriginal South Australia, Wilfrid Prest (ed.), *The Wakefield Companion to South Australian History*, Wakefield Press, Mile End, 2001, p. 9.

2 Several good books about Flinders have recently appeared, e.g. Jean Fornasiero, Peter Monteath and John West-Sooby, *Encountering Terra Australis*, Wakefield Press, Mile End, 2004.

3 *Australian Dictionary of Biography (ADB)*, Vols 1 and 3. It has recently been suggested that the Eyre Highway connecting Western Australia with the eastern states via the Bight and the north of the Peninsula to Port Augusta should be called the Eyre-Wylie Highway (John Kinsella, 'Eyre-Wylie Highway', *The Monthly*, December 2012, pp. 61–63).

4 Rob Foster and Amanda Nettelbeck, *Out of the Silence: The history and memory of South Australia's frontier wars*, Wakefield Press, Mile End, 2012; *ADB*, Vol. 1.

5 On the Hack family, see *ADB* Vol. l (J.B. Hack) and Vol. 4 (Wilton Hack) and most recently Iola Hack Mathews and Chris Durant, *Chequered Lives: John Barton Hack and Stephen Hack and the early days of South Australia*, Wakefield Press, Mile End, 2013. Re Yardea Station, see map, Google, and Sue Kneebone and Philip Jones, 'Naturally Disturbed', SASA Gallery, Adelaide, 2010.

6 Frank Masters, *Saga of Wangaraleednie: A story of early days on Eyre Peninsula. Franklin Harbour, South Australia*, Mail Newspapers, Adelaide, c. 1947.

7 Ronald Parsons, *Southern Passages: A maritime history of South Australia*, Wakefield Press, Mile End, 1986, p. 8; C.R. Twidale, M.J. Tyler and

M. Davies (eds), *Natural History of Eyre Peninsula*, Royal Society of South Australia, 1985, p. 2; Russel Ward, *The Australian Legend*, OUP, Melbourne, 1958, p. 8; H.P. Moore, 'Notes on the early settlers of South Australia prior to 1836', Royal Geographical Society of Australasia (SA Proceedings), 1924–1925, p. 87.

8 Port Germein jetty: 1676 metres at maximum length (Google ref, accessed 10/1/2013). Port Bonython, Moomba natural gas, oil and naphtha outlet located north of Whyalla, is now the longest jetty in SA (2400 metres).

9 Responsibility for jetties is a complicated question, but it seems from the SA History Hub the responsible body at that time was the SA Department of Marine and Harbors.

10 Russel Ward, *A Radical Life*, Macmillan, South Melbourne, 1988, pp. 81–82.

11 For more on the Gulf Trip see Parsons, *Port Lincoln Shipping*, printed and published by the author, 1981, p. 38.

12 For references see n. 14.

13 Eric Newby, *The Last Great Grain Race*, Picador, London, 1956, recounts 18-year-old Newby's experience as a hand on the largest of the ships in that race, the *Moshulu*, including a weekend in Port Lincoln with a local named Jack.

14 Mudamuckla: Peter Knife, *Peninsula Pioneer: A history of the railways on Eyre Peninsula*, Wahroonga, 2006, Appendix A; 'A Fair Exchange? Telecom pulls the plug on party lines', *Weekend Australian*, 24–25 October, 1987, p. 3.

15 'Ship stranded on S.A. Island [N. Neptune]', *Advertiser*, 26 January, 1959, p. 1; *Encyclopedia of Australian Shipwrecks* (accessed 12/1/2013); 'Lighthouses', *Wakefield Companion*, and Ronald Parsons, *Lighthouses of South Australia*, the author, Magill, 1985.

16 Knife, *Peninsula Pioneer*, postscript and p. 53.

17 Jim Fitzpatrick, *The Bicycle and the Bush: Man and the machine in rural Australia*, 1980, covers the period.

18 Her life is recorded in the *ADB* and she appears in the bicentennial publication *200 Australian Women.*

19 At the time of writing, Premier Stateliner provides services to Eyre Peninsula, from Adelaide to Port Lincoln and to Ceduna via Wudinna.

20 Robert Bedford, birth name Buddicom, see *ADB* Vol. 7.

Chapter 2 ~ Country life

1 D. Aitkin, '"Countrymindedness": The spread of an idea', in S.L. Goldberg and F.B. Smith (eds), Cambridge University Press, Melbourne, 1988, p. 115.

2 Rob Linn, *Battling the Land: 200 years of rural Australia*, Allen & Unwin, Sydney, 1999, p. 172 (broadacre farms); Don Aitkin, 'Return to Countrymindedness', in Graeme Davison and Marc Brodie (eds), *Struggle Country: The rural ideal in twentieth century Australia*, Monash University ePress, Melbourne, 2005, p. 172.

3 D.W. Meinig, *On the Margins of the Good Earth: The South Australian wheat frontier 1869–1884,* Rigby, Adelaide, 1962, 1970, and J.B. Hirst, *Adelaide and the Country 1870–1917: Their social and political relationship*, Melbourne University Press, Melbourne, 1973, are the classic studies.

4 Centrex mining company website, 2008, accessible from http//www.centrexmetals.com.au; Business Monthly, *The Advertiser*, August 2011, pp. 8–9.

5 Judith Brettt, *Quarterly Essay* 42, 2011, p. 56. I have since addressed this question in part in a contribution to *Adelaide: A literary city*, University of Adelaide Press, Adelaide, 2014.

6 George Woodroofe Goyder, (1826–1898) was surveyor general of South Australia 1861–1894, *ADB*; Judith Jeffrey, 'Goyder's Line', in *Wakefield Companion*, p. 232; Janis Sheldrick, *Nature's Line: George Goyder, surveyor, environmentalist, visionary*, Wakefield Press, Mile End, 2013.

7 Neville Collins, *The Jetties of South Australia: Past and present*, Neville Collins, Adelaide, 2005, p. 41; 'Nuyts, Pieter (1598–1659), mariner', *ADB: Supplement*, Melbourne University Press, Melbourne, 2005, and online.

8 K.S. Inglis, *The Stuart Case*, Melbourne University Press, Melbourne, 1961.

9 Elizabeth Salter, *Daisy Bates*, Cowan, McCann & Geoghegan, New York, 1972, pp. 243–245; Bob Reece, *Daisy Bates: Grand dame of the desert*, National Library of Australia, Canberra, 2007, p. 147, and SA hotel websites; M.E. Fenton, *W.K. Mallyon 1850–1933: A sketchbook of early church architecture in the mid north of South Australia*, Libraries Board of South Australia, Adelaide, 1971.

10 Robert Foster, Rick Hosking and Amanda Nettelbeck, *Fatal Collisions: The South Australian frontier of violence and memory,* Wakefield Press, Mile End, 2001, ch. 4, 'Recalling the Elliston Incident'; 'Gallery in the open Eyre', *SA*

Life, Dec 2006–Jan 2007, pp. 36–38; *Pioneer Stories by Ellen Liston*, comp. E.A. Harwood, Hassell Press, Adelaide, 1936.

11 For the Mortlock family, see *ADB*, Vol. 5 and 11; Eyre Peninsula is now third favourite tourist destination for South Australians.

12 Hematite: the mineral form of iron oxide, from black to red in colour.

13 Geoffrey Speirs, 'Museums', in *Wakefield Companion*, p. 232.

14 Bedford, Robert, born Buddicomb, 1874–1951, *ADB* Vol. 7.

15 For the Elliston mural, see *Fatal Collisions*, p. 44.

16 John Pickard, 'Lines across the Landscape: History, impact and heritage of Australian rural fences', PhD thesis, Macquarie University, 2010, p. 353.

17 Dobbins interview, 29 July 2011; Jennifer A. Jones, 'Old Age in a Young Colony: Image and experience in South Australia in the nineteenth century', PhD thesis, University of Adelaide, 2010.

18 Callen and Heathcote, in *Wakefield Companion*, pp. 266–267; Jill Roe, *Stella Miles Franklin: A life*, HarperCollins Australia, Pymble, 2008, p. 11.

19 The folk migration has yet to be studied in any detail. Sources include 'Effie' [Mrs John Durdin], *Pioneering days: Koppio 1903*, 8 pp., n.d., National Trust of South Australia, Tumby Bay Branch, c. 2000; see also Jill Roe, 'Belly-dancing in the Bush and other strategies for survival', *AHA Bulletin*, December 1998, pp. 14–17 (edited, Chapter 8 below).

20 *Souvenir of the Opening of the Tod River Water Scheme*, Thevenard, June 1928, SA Govt Printer, 1928.

21 Robert Murray, *Sandbelters: Memoirs of Middle Australia*, Arcadia, Melbourne, 2011, p. 24; Penelope Hetherington, *The Making of a Labor Politician: Family and politics in South Australia, 1900–1980,* published by the author, Perth, 1982.

22 Daphne Freeman (ed., *Eyre Peninsula Ramblings*, Lutheran Publishing House, Adelaide, 1985.

23 'The Yallunda Flat Store' in *Gum Trees and Gullies* (1986) refers to Bolah Shah as an Indian hawker who erected a shop at Yallunda Flat, apparently superseded in 1907 when a general store was built by the showground turn off by Messrs Walkom and Walters, p. 25.

24 Marianne Hammerton, *Water South Australia: A history of the Engineering and Water Supply Department,* Wakefield Press, Mile End, 1986, p. 188.

25 Data from the SA Genealogical Society website and certificates in my possession.

26 Letter in my possession.

27 Peter Stanley, *Whyalla at War*, City of Whyalla, Whyalla, 2004, p. 9. The population of Whyalla increased dramatically between 1937 and 1944 from c. 1350 to 7900.

28 Richard Waterhouse, *The Vision Splendid: A social and cultural history of rural Australian*, Curtin University Books, Fremantle Arts Centre Press, Perth, 2005; Bill Gammage, *The Biggest Estate on Earth: How Aborigines made Australia*, Allen & Unwin, Sydney, 2011; Heather Goodall, 'Telling Country: Memoir, modernity and narratives in rural Australia', *History Workshop Journal*, Spring 1999, 47, pp. 160–190.

29 Charles Fahey, '"A Splendid Place for a Home": The long history of the Australian family farm', in Alan Mayne and Stephen Atkinson (eds), *Outside Country: Histories of inland Australia*, Wakefield Press, Mile End, 2011.

30 Rob Linn, *Battling the Land*, Allen & Unwin, Sydney, 1999, p. 172.

31 Brett, *Quarterly Essay*, 2011; Jill Roe, 'Voluntary Action and the Rural Poor in the Age of Globalisation', in *Beveridge and Voluntary Action in Britain and the Wider British World*, Melanie Oppenheimer and Nicholas Deakin (eds), Manchester University Press, Manchester, 2011.

32 John Hirst, 'The Pioneer Legend', *[Australian] Historical Studies*, Vol. 18, No. 71, 1978, reprinted in his *Sense and Nonsense in Australian History*, 2005.

Chapter 3 ~ Water as a vital resource

1 'Magarey, Thomas (1825–1902)', *ADB* Vol. 2.

2 Port Lincoln was declared a city in 1971.

3 Eyre, Edward John (1815–1901), *ADB* Vol. 2; also Geoffrey Dutton, *The Hero as Murderer: The Life of Edward John Eyre, Australian Explorer and Governor of Jamaica*, Collins/Cheshire, Sydney and Melbourne, 1967, pp. 67–68.

4 Ibid; Robert Tod, 'Port Lincoln: A report', *Royal South Australian Almanack*, 1840.

5 *The Rose on the Sheep's Back: St Margaret's Anglican Church, Tumby Bay, including the Church of the Epiphany, Lipson – Celebrating 100 years in 2008*, the Congregation, printed Port Neill, SA, n.d..

6 'Goyder, George William (1826–1898)', 'Little Energy', *ADB*.

7 The Tod Reservoir was closed off between 2002 and 2004 due to salinity and agricultural chemicals in the water but remains part of the region's water supply back-up system, and it seems possible that it may be re-opened.

8 *Robert Bedford of Kyancutta*, comp. Sylvia Laube, Wednesday Press, Norwood, 1990, pp. 34, 31.

9 First Report, p. 1.

10 Jill Bowen, *Kidman: The forgotten king*, Fourth Estate, Sydney, 2007 edn, pp. 281–282; 'Joseph Timms', *Obituaries Australia* online; Souvenir Opening of the Tod River Scheme, 1928, SLSA.

11 *The History of Tumby Bay and District*, the Council, Tumby Bay, 1981, pp. 20–21.

12 *We Survived*, National Trust of South Australia (Tumby Bay Branch), n.d. (1960s?), notes significant seasonal variations.

13 The Centrex website has details.

14 Peter Treloar is MP for the state electorate of Flinders.

Chapter 4 ~ The school bus

1 State support for school buses came in Australia in the late 1930s, partly to encourage students to stay on in stressed rural areas. Craig Campbell and Helen Proctor, *A History of Australian Schooling*, Allen & Unwin, Sydney, 2014, p. 159.

2 Hank Nelson, *With Its Hat about Its Ears: Recollections of the bush school*, ABC Enterprises, Crows Nest, 1989, pp. 96–97; Colin Thiele, *Grains of Mustard Seed*, ABC Enterprises, Crows Nest, 1975, p. 157, 180; *Voice from the Past: The life and letters of Joseph William Blumson, 1881–1937*, University of South Australia, Adelaide, 2001, p. 270.

3 Harry Schiller recollections, n.d. [1990s?], transcript in my possession, p. 3, courtesy Amanda Nettelbeck.

4 Kay Whitehead and Ben Wadham, 'Marking a Marginal Past: Schooling and dispossession in the Franklin Harbour district', *History Australia*, 8, 3, December 2011, pp. 39–40.

5 Turner Hospital's recollections are excerpted in the *Oxford Book of Australian School Days* (1997), as are mine.

6 Christina Ross to Amanda Nettelback, 1996, transcript in my possession, courtesy Amanda Nettelbeck, and 'Eight years at Chandada', n.d., transcript in my possession, courtesy Penelope Hetherington.

7 Whitehead and Whadham, 'Marking a Marginal Past', pp. 39–40.

8 Nelson, *With Its Hat about Its Ears*, p. 199.

Chapter 5 ~ 'Farming is fun': A child's perspective

1 Graeme Leech, 'Will we still have . . . sheepdogs', *The Australian* supplement, *A Vision for the Nation's Future*, pt 11, 2006.

Chapter 6 ~ 'We plough the fields and scatter': Church and community

1 Hymn no. 963, *The Methodist Hymnal*, London, 8th edn, 1962.

2 Helen Caterer, *Australian Outback: Sixty years of Bush Church Aid*, Anglican Information Office, Sydney, 1981, also *BCA: 75 years not out*, BCA, Sydney, 2000, and *ADB*, Vol. 8; Robert J. Scrimgeour, *Some Scots Were Here: A history of the Presbyterian Church in South Australia 1839–1977*, Lutheran Publishing House, Adelaide, 1986, p. 106.

3 S.G. Forth, *Methodism on Eyre Peninsula: A lecture*, 1956, p. 7. Tumby Mission, established in 1906, then consisted of six preaching places: Tumby, Lipson, Stokes, Hillside, Roeville, and Cummins.

4 George Wilfred Scholefield (1886–1969), Ken and Leonie Cable, *Clerical Index* (online) and *Port Lincoln Times*, 12 May 1933, p. 9; Scholefield typescript, n.d. (c. 1964), and Wendy Treloar et al., *Cummins: Its people and history*, Adelaide, a bicentennial project, n.d., (c. 1988).

5 Th. Hebart, *The United Evangelical Lutheran Church in Australia*, Lutheran Publishing House, Adelaide, 1938; ms. chart, n.d., Lutheran Church Archives, Adelaide.

6 Frank Walker, *Maralinga*, Adelaide, 2014; Rebecca Grigg, 'Nuclear literature after Maralinga', in Tanya Dalziell and Paul Genoni (eds), *Telling Stories: Australian life and literature 1935–2012*, Clayton, 2013.

7 C.V. Eckermann, *The Mission and the Nunga People*, Openbook, Adelaide, 2010. I thank the South Australian Archivist of the Lutheran Church for information about Yalata.

8 Helen McCormack, *By Horse and Buggy: History of the Catholic parish of Port Lincoln 1869–1986*, Port Lincoln, 1986, and 'The History of St Mary of the Angels Catholic Church', pamph., comp. Helen McCormack, Port

Lincoln, 1986; Margaret Press, *From Our Broken Toil: South Australian Catholics 1836 to 1905*, Vol. 1, p. 230, *Colour and Shadow*, South Australian Catholics 1906–1992, Vol. 2, pp. 72–73, Vol. 1, p. 230.

9 SA Methodist Conference Minutes, 1960, p. 13. I thank David Hilliard and Dean Drayton for statistical data.

10 Bill and Maureen Nosworthy, *Tjeiringa: The story of Sheringa district*, Sheringa, 1988, Methodist church est. 1900 demolished 1973, pp. 186, 190–192.

11 *The Rose on the Sheep's Back: St Margaret's Anglican Church, Tumby Bay, including the Church of the Epiphany, Lipson*, n.p., Port Neill, 2008.

12 'The guide to the papers of the Australian National University Survey of War Memorials', Series 6, Australian War Memorial, 2010, lists twenty war memorials on Eyre Peninsula.

Chapter 7 ~ 'I danced for the Queen': Exuberance and otherwise in regional history since the 1950s

1 *Port Lincoln Times,* 25 March, 1954, p. 1.

2 *The Royal Tour of Australia and New Zealand in Pictures*, Herald and Sun-News Pictorial, Melbourne, 1954, unpaginated (c. p. 70).

3 Illuminated Address of Welcome, postcard in my possession.

4 'Queen pays tribute to pioneering spirit', *Port Lincoln Times*, 25 March, 1954, p. 1.

5 *Royal Visit to Australia of Her Majesty Queen Elizabeth II and His Royal Highness the Duke of Edinburgh 1954*, Department of the Interior, Canberra, 1954, pp. 30, 90–91; Adelaide *Advertiser*, 24 April, 1954, p. 1, 9.

6 Miss J.C. West to Mrs J.H. Randall, Port Lincoln, 10 March, 1994, letter in my possession, courtesy Mrs Randall.

7 'Queen delighted by children's display', *Port Lincoln Times*, 25 March, 1954, p. 1.

8 '1000 ex-servicemen expected here next Saturday', *Port Lincoln Times*, 18 May, 1954, p. 1. I thank Pat Green for advice re the Port Lincoln war memorial.

9 'Royal visit was a masterpiece of cooperation' and 'Nobody fainted at Port Lincoln', *Port Lincoln Times*, 25 March, 1954, inner pages.

10 'The mayor's message', *Port Lincoln Times*, 18 March, 1954, p. 1; Jane Connors, 'The Royal Tour of Australia', *Aust. Hist. Studs*, 25, 100, 1993, pp. 371–382.

11 *Programme for the Visit to Australia of Her Majesty The Queen and His Royal Highness the Duke of Edinburgh, 3rd February to 1st April 1954* has the official itinerary (2nd edn January 1954, Mitchell Library).

12 A local title seen subsequently is *Poppies in the Wheat: Pioneers, Kyancutta, and the McKennas – the memories of Kath Hunt as told to Craig Hunt*, Venatus Pty Ltd, Melbourne, 2004.

13 Jill Roe, 'Miles Franklin and 1890s Goulburn', *Aust. Lit. Studs*, 20, 4, 2002, pp. 359–369.

14 Jill Roe, 'Belly-dancing in the bush and other strategies for survival', *Aust. Hist. Assocn Bulletin* December 1998, pp. 12–24 and Chapter 8; *Stella Miles* Franklin, pp. 60–61, 144–145.

Chapter 8 ~ The Show

1 Re 1903, presumably this was a preview; the Roe family arrived via Tumby Bay to settle in 1905, as documented in Anna Roe's diary.

2 I thank Les Heathcote for help with census data.

3 Michael Williams, *The Making of the South Australian Landscape*, 1974, p. 37.

4 *The History of Tumby Bay and District*, 1981.

5 *Gum Trees and Gullies*, p. 112.

Chapter 9 ~ Survival: The Aboriginal experience

1 Dylan Coleman, *Mazin Grace*, UQP, St Lucia, 2012, a fictionalised account of her mother's early years on Koonibba Mission, won the David Unaipon Award for Indigenous writing in 2011; Robert Foster and Amanda Nettelbeck, *Out of the Silence: The history and memory of South Australia's frontier wars*, Wakefield Press, Mile End, 2012.

2 *Encyclopedia of Aboriginal Australia*, 1994, Vol. 2; Robert Foster and Tom Gara, 'Aboriginal Culture in South Australia', *The Flinders History of South Australia: Social history*, 1986, p. 65; Philip Jones, *Ochre and Rust*, Wakefield Press, Mile End, 2007, p. 333; H.P. Moore, 'Notes on the early settlers of South Australia prior to 1836', Royal Geographical Society of Australasia (SA Proceedings), 1924–1925, p. 87; a convict presence, Rebe Taylor,

Unearthed: The Aboriginal Tasmanians of Kangaroo Island, Wakefield Press, Mile End, 2002, p. 52.

3 Jean Fornasiero, Peter Monteath and John West-Sooby, *Encountering Terra Australis: The Australian Voyages of Nicolas Baudin and Matthew Flinders*, Wakefield Press, Mile End, pp. 133–134.

4 Josephine Flood, *The Original Australians: Story of the Aboriginal people*, 2006, p. 169; for information on fishing methods, e.g. the training of dugongs at Proper Bay near Port Lincoln and fish traps at Dutton Bay inlet, *ibid.*, p. 160, and graphic, Chapter 1.

5 Christobel Mattingley and Ken Hampton, *Survival in Our Own Land*, p. 268, 307 and *ADB* Vol. 17, pp. 481–482; Adele Pring (ed.), *Women of the Centre*, 1990, pp. 48–66; 'Nungas' is the term preferred by Aboriginal people in *Survival in Our Own Land*. It derives from the Wirangu word *Nhangga*.

6 Ngingali Cullen was born at Ooldea Soak and died in Canberra, *Australian Women's Register*, http://www.womenaustralia.info/biogs/AWE4893b.htm, accessed 21/8/2013.

7 Judith Raftery, *Not Part of the Public: Non-Indigenous policies and practices and the health of Indigenous South Australians 1836–1973*, Wakefield Press, Mile End, 2006, p. 262; *Black to White*, Appendix 1 (1947 census), total 4196; *Australians: Historical statistics* (1987), p. 4. *The Flinders History of South Australia*, Table 7.3, p. 178, gives the enumerated Aboriginal population for 1901 as 3888 and an estimated minimum Aboriginal population for that year as 4888, and the enumerated Aboriginal population for 1954 as 3212 (no estimates are given for the intervening period, nor an estimated minimum Aboriginal population for 1954).

8 Not to be confused with Carlton and Adelaide Football Club player Eddie Betts, who also hails from Eyre Peninsula.

9 Royal Commission into Aboriginal Deaths in Custody. Report of the inquiry into the death of Edward Frederick Betts, to the Government of South Australia, 1991 (http://www.austlii.edu.au/au/other/IndigLRes/rciadic/individual/brm_efb). Elliott Johnston (1918–2011) was a judge in the Supreme Court of SA 1983–1988.

10 Tom Gara, 'Aboriginal–European Frontier Conflict', *Wakefield Companion*, pp. 1–2; Susan Marsden and John Dallwitz, *Summary Report: Identification of sites, routes and reports representing early European contacts with South*

Australia, 1981, pp. 10–29; Robert Foster and Amanda Nettelbeck, *Out of the Silence*, 2012, ch. 3; J.D. Somerville, 'Early Days of Eyre Peninsula: Disappearance of Dutton and party', *Port Lincoln Times*, 7/2/1936, p. 3.

11 Foster and Nettelbeck, *ibid.*; Clamor Schurmann (1815–1893), Lutheran missionary, *ADB: Supplement*.

12 John Charles Darke (1802–1844), *ADB* Vol. 1; John Summers, 'Colonial Race Relations', *The Flinders History of South Australia: Social history,* 1986, p. 301.

13 Matthew Blagden Hale (1811–1895) became first Anglican bishop of Perth in 1857, *ADB*, Vol. 4.

14 Peggy Brock and Doreen Kartinyeri, *Poonindie: The rise and destruction of an Aboriginal agricultural community*, 1989.

15 *Across the Bar to Waterloo Bay: Elliston 1878–1978*, Elliston Centenary Book Committee, 1978, pp. 9–10; 'A Not so Innocent Vision: Re-visiting the literary works of Ellen Liston, Jane Sarah Doudy and Myrtle Rose White (1838–1961)', Janette Helen Hancock, PhD thesis, University of Adelaide, 2007.

16 *Out of the Silence*, p. 86.

17 Rick Hosking, 'Ellen Liston's "Doctor" and the Elliston Incident', in Philip Butterss ed., *Essays in South Australian Writing*, 1995, p. 63; *Pioneers: Stories by Ellen Liston*, comp. E.A. Harwood, Hassell Press, Adelaide, 1936, contains several items that refer to the area, including the undated short story 'Lucy and I'; Hancock, PhD thesis, University of Adelaide.

18 With regards to 'it tells both ways', see e.g. *Across the Bar*, pp. 6–7 on the killing of shepherds.

19 C.V. Eckerman, *Koonibba: The Mission and the Nunga People*, 2010; regarding self-government, a Community Council was established in 1967, and full control gained in 1972, *Water Supply and Use in Aboriginal Communities in South Australia*, Dept of Aboriginal Affairs and Reconciliation, Adelaide, c. 2004, p. 129.

20 *Water Supply and Use,* p. 130.

21 Bob Reece, *Daisy Bates: Grand dame of the desert*, NLA Canberra, 2007, pp. 7, 146–150, 124–125. Bates was born in Ireland on 16 October 1859, some three years earlier than previously thought (Reece, p. 13). She does not mention Eyre Peninsula in her book.

22 *Saga of Wangaraleednie*, pp. 20–21; Kay Whitehead and Ben Wadham, 'Marking a Marginal Past: Schooling and dispossession in the Franklin Harbour District', *History Australia* 8, 3, December 2011, p. 29.

23 *Franklin Harbour District Council 1888–1988,* [c. 1988]; Willshire *ADB,* Vol. 12; Amanda Nettelbeck and Robert Foster, *In the Name of the Law*, 2007, pp. 163–164; Schiller transcript, p. 6 ('quite a few'). Apparently there was contrasting police behaviour at Tumby Bay c. 1914, but I have not been able to find the evidence.

24 K.S. Inglis, *The Stuart Case*, 1961. Stuart was born 1932 at the Jay Creek government reserve west of Alice Springs.

25 Missionaries of the Sacred Heart website, 24 November 2014.

26 Native title applications (registered and unregistered) 30 June 2012, *Annual Report*, SA National Title Services, 2012 (website); 'Barngarla people granted partial native title over large area of SA Eyre Peninsula', ABC News website, 28 January 2015 (with map).

27 Rex Battarbee (1893–1973), *ADB* Vol. 13 and *Modern Australian Aboriginal Art*, 1951.

28 Lois Healy and Jennie Strickland, pers. comm., Adelaide, 27 April 2013.

Chapter 10 ~ Since the 1960s

1 As far as I am aware the word Indigenous came into wider usage in the late 20th century.

2 I thank Bill Gunson, now retired from Macquarie University Library, for assistance with census data.

3 Michael Sexton, 'About Townies', in *Footy Town: Stories of Australia's game*, eds Paul Daffey and John Harms, Malarkey Publications, Fitzroy North, 2013, pp. 235–236.

4 Georgine W. Clarsen, 'The Flip Side: Women in the Redex Around Australia Reliability Trials of the 1950s', *Humanities Research*, xvii, 2, 2011.

5 The findings of a Coronial Inquest were handed down on 18 December 2007 and a summary and the full document may be consulted on the South Australian Government website under Fire and Emergency Services Commission, also accessed under the subject heading Wangary Bushfires.

6 *Port Lincoln Times,* editorial 20 January 2005.

7 Stanley Robb/Jill Roe, by phone, 7 July 2014.

INDEX

Y

Wakefield Press is an independent publishing and distribution company based in Adelaide, South Australia. We love good stories and publish beautiful books. To see our full range of books, please visit our website at www.wakefieldpress.com.au where all titles are available for purchase.

Find us!

Twitter: www.twitter.com/wakefieldpress
Facebook: www.facebook.com/wakefield.press
Instagram: instagram.com/wakefieldpress